BEYOND COURAGE

Shipwrecked and Adrift;
One Family Fights To Survive

by

Robert Aros

with Rob Ternan

Shore Publishing
Long Beach, California

Published by: Shore Publishing

239 Nieto Avenue, Suite A

Long Beach, CA 90803-5502

Library of Congress Cataloging in Publication Data

Aros, Robert C.

Beyond Courage / Robert Aros with Rob Ternan.

p. cm.

1. Survival after airplane accidents, shipwrecks, etc. 2. Aros family. I. Ternan, Rob. II. Title.

G525.A767 1994   910.4'5   93–086679

QBI93—22278

ISBN 0-9638704-0-8 Hardcover

Printed in the United States.

PERMISSIONS ACKNOWLEDGEMENTS

A special thanks to Leonard Tolhurst, Colin Busch and all the Ham Radio Operators, without who's efforts this story would not be told. Also to the many who had a share in our rescue.

Thanks to Rob Ternan who's education and expertise in the literary field made this book possible.

Grateful acknowledgement is made to the following for permission to reprint previously published material.

American Medical Association Encyclopedia of Medicine: by American Medical Association Copyright © 1989 By Dorling Kindersley Ltd. and the American Medical Association. Reprinted by permission of Random House, Inc.

The Merck Manual of Diagnosis & Therapy, Edition 16, pp88, 955 &956, edited by Robert Berkow © 1992 by Merck & Co., Inc., Rahway, NJ

The World Book Encyclopedia, 1993 Edition: World Book Inc., 1993

National Geographic, "Wind, Wave, Star, and Bird", Dec. 1974; and "El Nino's Ill Wind", Feb.1984

Are You Confused?, Paavo Airola, Ph.D: Health Plus Publishers, Sherwood, OR, 1980

*The Yearbook,*1982: Watchtower Bible and Tract Society, 1981

Seabirds of the World, Eric Hosking and Ronald Lockley, Facts on File Inc., 1983

Letter by Leonard Tolhurst: April 1993

Audio letter by Colin Busch: January, 1983

Photos courtesy of Fiji Times

Dedicated to my lovely wife Margaret,
who has always been to me more than a wife,
but a true friend and partner through the sea of life.

PREFACE

I cannot remember a time when I did not have the dream. It seems now that it was with my life's very first gasps of air that I breathed in images of a place called the South Pacific, and with it the obsession that someday I would get there. Island-green, ocean-blue, beach-sand-white—those were the colors I saw when I closed my eyes.

By age forty-nine, the fantasy had hardly dimmed at all. If anything, it seemed closer, more focused, almost within my grasp. The rigors of a failed first marriage and demands of raising a family were behind me. I had money in the bank, and came to believe that the South Pacific could be transformed—from escapist dream to life-changing inevitability.

Still at home with me was my youngest son, Christian, age sixteen. We had been joined by my beloved second wife, Margaret. Together, we giggled like kids the day we bought a 36-foot sloop called *Vamonos* (Spanish for "let's go!"). After rigging her for long-distance cruising, we joyously slipped out of Long Beach Harbor on December 1, 1981. An eight-day shake-down cruise brought us to Cabo San Lucas in Mexico. There we met hundreds of kindred spirits, "yachties" like us bound for ports of the imagination from the South Pacific, to the Caribbean.

Our ties with this community of wandering water gypsies were immediate and deep. We helped each other with boat repairs, swapped facts and salty tales of sea adventures, and devised out navigation plans for an ocean crossing. Five blissful months later, we set sail for the Marquesas in French Polynesia.

The twenty-five day voyage was everything a fantasy-come-true should be. The weather was beautiful, the ship handled like a dream, and the sights we drank in were beyond the colors of even my imagination. The Marquesas... the Tuamotus... Tahiti... places with exotic dream names became the real images of swaying palm, beaches of white or black sands, balmy trade winds. Even the natives were friendly!

Five months slipped past like a soaring albatross. We then set sail for Rarotonga in the Cook Islands, with plans to rendezvous with friends in New Zealand. The fantasy was continuing, and I had begun to get comfortable with its gentle rhythms. But it was there, somewhere beyond Rarotonga that the dream ended.

What follows is reality—the thoughts, the words, the events, the fears recounted here reflect what we today, to the best of out recollections, have been able to distill from records, memories and the nightmares of that life-shattering experience.

What remains for our family is the legacy of those days, the hard-earned lessons we learned about life, love, faith, and the deepest secrets of the human heart. There in the angry waters beyond Rarotonga, we were driven beyond help, beyond hope, even beyond courage. This is the story that survives.

—Robert Aros, 1993

ONE

My slumber was shattered as a loud crack filled my ears. I felt myself airborne, but the flight from my berth to the floor was short and the landing hard. In an instant, the insult was echoed as a hailstorm of books pelted me.

"Was that a whale? Did a whale just hit us ?!" yelled my seventeen year-old son, Chris. His words echoed around in my befuddled brain.

Something is not right! I thought. We're leaning hard to port!

Still groggy, I stumbled to my feet. I was naked, but heedlessly scrambled up the steps to the cockpit. Something was desperately wrong!

Topside, Margaret was at the starboard rail, staring over the side into the darkness.

"What happened?" I demanded.

She didn't answer, but continued her glassy-eyed stare into the unknown. Despite a dizzying forty-five degree list, I turned back to the wheel and unfastened its lock. I tried to spin the wheel to the starboard, but it wouldn't budge. Suddenly, the whole boat leapt backward and crashed down hard. I tried the wheel again, and this time it spun easily. Too Easily. A sickening realization hit me—the rudder's not in the water!

I stumbled back to Margaret's side and peered into the darkness. The overcast skies were admitting little light, but I could hear the crashing of the waves below. I could just make out the phosphorescence of their white caps. Just then, the moon broke through.

Now I could see the waves, and make out what it was they were striking. It was solid ground! We were perched on a reef!

Another big wave hit, and the boat skidded backward two or three feet. I realized that when we hit, we had spun around and were now facing the way we'd come. Another wave drove us back again. With each wave, we were being shoved backwards, but toward what? Toward the edge of the deep, came the sobering realization. But what then? Could we survive what was coming? Were we still seaworthy?

Chris appeared at the top of the ladder. "What is it?" he asked. There was fear in his voice. "What's happened to us? What are we going to do?" His innocent, trusting eyes demanded an answer. But what could I say?

My brain was still clumsily trying to grasp our situation. I'm the captain! But what should I do? Our lives are in my hands. I must do the right thing! But my confidence was shaken. How did we go so wrong? Did I miscalculate? How could this happen to my fantasy?!

TWO

We strained our bodies against the force of the hairpin curve. As the rickety old van clumsily found its footing and chugged up the road, a chorus of "Whoas!" assaulted me from the back seat.

"Hey, I thought you said mountain climbing was safe!" Tom chided me in mock concern. His wife, Mary, gleefully joined in the fun.

"Now, Tom! Bob was only talking about climbing up the mountain. He didn't say anything about the drive up here!"

We had grown to cherish the company of fellow yachties like Tom and Mary, who had joined us for the day with Dave and Jan. They were all in their twenties and full of optimism. We had easily become friends months before in

Cabo San Lucas. Such relationships had blossomed into one of the real unanticipated joys of our planned two-year hiatus in the South Pacific. Ten months from home we relied on this close community of wandering sea-gypsies especially at sea.

"Will you listen to this, Margaret?" I shot back, playing along. "These folks get picked up this morning, in style! Then, we chauffeur them around a beautiful island, show them all the sights..."

"And all they do," Margaret jumped in with a wink, shaking her blonde, curly hair, " is complain about your absolutely perfect driving! Well, I think you should stop right now and let all four of them out right here!"

"Hey! Wait a minute!" Dave interjected. Even at play, he had a lawyer's sense of positioning that revealed his law school education and the law career awaiting him back home. "Jan and I were just sitting here thinking what a great driver Bob is! Weren't we, babe?" he purred insincerely.

Jan was quick to take his cue. "Yes, and of course, we're wild about the lovely interior of this vintage... or should I say, classic van!" she gushed.

I looked back over my shoulder and grinned. "Okay! Okay! Sorry about the rough ride. But you've got to agree—we were fortunate to borrow this van at all. I mean, foolish me! I totally forgot to pack my car on the sloop!"

"Yeah, it's always the little things you forget," Dave cracked.

We all laughed, except Chris, my seventeen year-old son. He hadn't said two words all morning, but just sat there in the front seat like a curled-up thunderhead. It was clear on his face that he wanted to be anywhere—except with us. Such sullenness was unusual. His short build and Michael J. Fox face was normally complemented by an eagerness to please.

Seven years before, a bruising divorce had shattered our family of five children. Chris, the youngest at age ten, had become my best buddy and roommate. During the first months of my bachelorhood, terrible fits of weeping often overtook me. But Chris would come to me and push the corners of my mouth up with his slender fingers, and with infectious innocence declare, "Smile, Daddy! Everything's going to be okay!"

Later, I met and married the vivacious Margaret, almost twenty years my junior at age twenty-four. She brought new joy into my life, as well as new strains on my relationship with my children. But on that sunny day in the Cook Islands, such concerns were half a world away and all but forgotten, or so I hoped.

On everyone's mind was the imminent voyage ahead. On separate days we all would sail our three vessels out of Rarotonga for New Zealand, some two weeks to the east. There, we'd sit out the hurricane season. I pulled over and parked the van. "Here we are, folks!" I announced. "the second highest peak on Rarotonga—Te Rua... What is it, honey?"

"Te Rua Manga Needle. One thousand, three hundred and fifty-five feet," Margaret declared authoritatively.

"How do you know that?" Dave said, cross-examining her.

"Because I bought the book!" she answered with a giggle.

"Ah, a reader!" he reflected. "Well, now we'll see if you two are climbers as well."

"Don't worry about us, Dave! We'll soon see who's huffing and puffing at the top!" I said, throwing down the gauntlet to the younger man.

He climbed out of the van and drank in the challenge before us. Everyone headed off toward the foot of the trail, except Chris and I. He had been the last to get out of the van.

"You're going to like this climb, Chris," I offered. "They say the views are incredible."

He frowned and answered glumly, "No kids, though."

"No, there's nobody exactly your age here, that's true," I began. "But Tom and Mary are in their twenty's and you like them. And Dave and Jan, too, right?"

Just then, Margaret returned to the van. "C'mon, you guys! You ready?"

Chris was ready, but only to let out his frustrations.

"You know, I like to mostly hang around with who I want to be with," he sputtered. "Not your friends! I mean, I don't even wanna be here! In Rarotonga, I mean!.."

"Well," Margaret began, trying to reason with him. "This is only a stop on the way to New Zealand, you know. We're just here to get our visas and everything..."

"I didn't like that we didn't stay in Tahiti!" Chris answered hotly. "You said we were gonna stay there for the hurricane season!"

Chris had met friends his own age there, and had obviously been fuming about having to leave them behind.

"Well, we changed our minds, Chris," Margaret answered in a tone that invoked an adult's authority over him. That seemed to gall Chris even more.

Jan and the others yelled to us, and asked if anything was wrong. I waved back and yelled that we'd be right there. Chris was ready for more.

"Yeah, you changed your minds! You and Dad! What about me? Who asked me? You know, Margaret, you should be smart enough to treat me with a little respect!" he snorted.

"That's enough, Chris!" I stepped in.

Once again, I was being called upon to play the role familiar to any parent who brings a new spouse into an existing family. I loved and respected my wife. I loved and respected my kids. All I ever wanted was for them to love and respect one another. But too often, resentment and hurt came to the surface, and I was forced to play umpire. It was a role I did not enjoy. I wanted to be done with this outburst, but Chris was not finished.

"You know, Margaret," he began bitterly, "you are not that much older than me! You're only thirty! And you certainly aren't my mother!"

"Chris, I said that's enough!" I declared forcefully.

Margaret was stunned, and fumbled shakily for an answer.

"Chris, I... I love you! All I want is for us to all be a family..." she began. But Chris pounced on her suggestion.

"Family! Hey! I'm not your fam-..." he blurted out as I cut him off.

"Enough! That's it!" I roared. My outburst froze Chris's words in mid-air.

Only once in my life had I ever struck Chris. That had been in Mexico months before when he had repeatedly sassed Margaret. Such disrespect had always been intolerable to me, so I had instinctively reached out and slapped his face. Now, suddenly, I felt like I was on the verge of doing it again, and I hated the thought. You can't beat love into a child. Besides, he was normally such a good kid— always positive, helpful, supportive. Maybe it was me. Maybe I was getting old. After all, I was fifty years old! But that's not that old. Not really.

I lowered my voice.

"Lookit! We're here! We're together! We're with friends! Can't we just have a good time?"

Chris glared at me, then moved on past. Margaret just stood there with deep pain contorting her pretty face.

"It's all right," I offered. She tried to smile, but I could tell she would mull over Chris's hurtful words with every step up Te Rua Manga Needle.

Soon we were on the trail. The first part is pretty easy, but the final leg becomes steep. All of it is incredibly beautiful. As you gain altitude, the surrounding jungle begins to open up. Lush, deep green vistas spread out before the eye, framed by the dazzling white of the beaches and pale aqua of the lagoon. Beyond the reef, the deep, deep blue of the sea reminds you that this is but a tiny speck of land poking tenuously above the vast, overpowering ocean.

We weren't the first people to have made the ascent, so the undergrowth was somewhat flattened as we shuttled along in our good walking shoes with day-packs on our backs. We soon fell into a single file as Tom led the way, followed by me, and then Margaret.

"Tom!" she called past me. "We're keeping the 'cockroach net' going on the way to New Zealand, right?"

As our radio operator, Margaret was the point of contact for our wide-ranging radio communications. The "cockroach net," so named for the large flying cockroaches native to the South Pacific, was our term for the informal radio network we had established among our three vessels. We all participate in the larger Pacific Maritime Net that included its base stations and many mobile units such as ours. But the more personal net among friends strengthened our sense of community, even at sea.

"Sure," answered Tom. "Dave and I already talked about keeping it up with you. You guys leaving tomorrow?"

"First light," I said.

"Well, we'll be a couple of days behind you then," he responded. "We're gonna 'buddy-boat.' Sure you guys don't want to wait and head out with us?"

"No, we'll leave tomorrow," I answered, stopping short. "Wow! Look at that!"

Between a stand of banana trees and a papaya tree, a vista opened up of Avatiu Harbor below. It was a vision of glittering turquoise all the way out to the reef. As we all stopped to take in the sight, a bottle-neck formed on the trail. Chris approached from behind, glanced out at the view, and kept walking.

"How many days do you figure to New Zealand, Bob?" Dave asked.

"Thirteen to fifteen, depending on the wind," I answered.

"Ho! Ho! Do you think your *Vamonos* is that much faster than our *Karana*?" he asked good-naturedly.

"The *Vamonos* has a good ten feet of length on the

Karana! I'd think something was really wrong if it weren't faster," I declared.

"A day faster maybe," Dave conceded. "Over two weeks. I was figuring the trip closer to fifteen to eighteen days."

"Well, we'll see," I allowed. "The wind's been strong all week."

The terrain ahead of us began to get steeper, and Tom, in the lead, scrambled up onto a large boulder.

"Mountain goat country," he declared, as he jumped from boulder to boulder up the hill.

"Hey, that looks like fun!" I declared, scrambling onto the first boulder.

Dave followed me, and we jumped from boulder to boulder.

"Hey, Chris! Come try this! It's good!" I yelled.

He looked up at me from his position just abreast of me, and decided to give it a try. He scurried up the boulder and joined in the romp.

I turned back and yelled. "Hey, Margaret! Girls! Try this!"

"I'm fine here," she declared. "We'll probably beat you to the top! You wanna bet?" she teased.

"I don't bet," I answered.

"Chicken!" she laughed.

During my drive back, I turned to the other couples. "We've been seeing a lot of the Rarotongan family—the Napas, and this afternoon they're going to take us out to their land. They want us to take some fresh fruit with us on our journey. If I know them, they'll load us down with more fruit than we can eat!"

"They've been so generous with us," Margaret added. "They just love to give."

"Some people are like that, givers," Mary nodded.

"Yes, they are wonderful people," I agreed. "So listen, we can't really say no to them about anything. But if they give us as much as I think they will, we want to give you all

some of it tomorrow before we leave. They have their own
banana trees and orange trees and papayas..."
  "And fresh honey, too!" Margaret chimed in.
  "That sounds really great!" Jan smiled.

THREE

"Sail a little to the left of the setting sun in November."

—Kupe, the Rarotongan, legendary discoverer of New Zealand, from his directions to his
decendants, National Geographic, December, 1974.

Leaving Rarotonga
November 7, 1982
Avatiu Harbor, Rarotonga
Aboard the Vamonos

The channel leaving Avatiu Harbor heads almost due north
through a narrow passage only sixty feet wide, so vessels
never leave under sail. We fired up the *Vamonos* engine and
slipped easily out of the lagoon through the pass. After
nearly a year at sea, we felt confident in our seamanship,
and slipped out to sea smoothly and efficiently.

After clearing the reef, the *Vamonos* settled into the gentle rise and fall of the giant Pacific swells. We swung around and took our course for the southwest. I turned the wheel over to Margaret and went forward to bend on the sails.

I felt wonderful. I was still wearing a lei around my neck as the fresh winds tossled my hair, and beckoned our family gently forward, into the friendly seas.

The mainsail was furled on its boom. Chris joined me for a quick swabbing of the deck to make sure no grime would get on the jib sail. Then, I dumped the jib out of its bag and began unfolding it. I took the corner called the tack, and walked it forward to the headstay where I fitted it onto the clevis pin. Chris hooked the forward part of the sail to the halyard, and we ran up the sheet using the rope that attached to the rear corner of the sail and ran through a pulley block and back to the cockpit.

When it was ready, we unfastened the straps that secured the furled mainsail, then flopped the whole thing to the leeward side of the boom, away from the wind.

"It's a good day, isn't it?" I smiled.

"The wind feels great!" Chris grinned back.

His natural good spirits were beginning to re-emerge, and I was glad. Still, I knew he and I would have to talk. I could tell he was still harboring ill feelings about our leaving Tahiti, but I was sure he would really enjoy New Zealand. He was usually happy wherever he was. Besides, we had all made a commitment to this two-year excursion around the Pacific. We were doing it together. That's how we had planned it....Well, at least, that's how Margaret and I had planned it. But Chris had agreed. Of course, maybe he was just being agreeable. Maybe he was having second thoughts. I had to get him alone. Maybe when Margaret was making dinner, we could find a few moments together. On a thirty-six foot sloop, privacy is a precious commodity that requires some logistical planning.

"Margaret! Say, Margaret!" I called back to her at the helm. "Yeah! You can cut the engine now!"

I felt the surge as the twenty-knot winds filled our fully-rigged sails. What a feeling. Here you are, standing on a boat. Your feet connect you with the deck, the deck is connected with the mast, the mast with the sails, and the sails with the wind, the very power of earth. Suddenly, it is that power that is carrying you in it's arms. There is nothing like it!

Sure, a motor is necessary for negotiating harbors or if you become becalmed. But ask a real sailor. He or she will tell you—there is no joy like killing the engine and feeling the power of the wind. Suddenly, that nagging industrial clatter is gone. It is just you and the sweet silence of a ship skimming the waves under sail. Before there were motors there was only the wind. It is the way it always was. It is the way it should always be.

Margaret slipped to my side. "I put out some fishing lines. Good chance something will strike this close to land."

"Fine. What's our heading?" I asked.

"We settled into 268 degrees after you secured the sheets," she answered.

"Hummm," I said, making some quick calculations. "I rigged us downwind so that means we are heading almost due west. You know, if we head straight out before the wind, instead of cutting back toward the southwest, that would mean a beautiful, smooth sail for two or three days. Then, we could head down. Maybe I should plot a new course."

"But then we'd be cutting more into the wind when we head southwest," she responded, "I mean, more than if we just headed southwest now, wouldn't we?"

"Oh, not that much more, honey. We'd be on a broad reach in either case. It'd just be a little less broad," I defended.

"Well," she shrugged. "Let's get out the chart".

I became convinced of the wisdom of my new plan as I worked it out on the chart. The original course would have taken us through open sea, passing south of two reefs called Haran and Beveridge. Then finally, almost to New Zealand, we'd end up north of the Kermadec Islands. My calculations had been based upon the prevailing wind and currents from Rarotonga to New Zealand which generally flow southwest. But now the wind had veered to almost due west. Why not take advantage of it?

In figuring course degrees, you begin by recognizing that a circle contains 360 degrees. Now imagine that the circle is the face of a clock. Place that clock face on the chart with north at the top. Looking clockwise, when you get to three o'clock, that's ninety degrees. Six o'clock is 180 degrees. Nine is 270 degrees. Since we were heading on a course of 268 degrees, that meant we were sailing almost due west.

After looking at the chart, it was clear that a heading of 268 degrees would allow us to clear the breakers, then, in a few days near the two reefs, we'd head southwesterly into New Zealand.

"What do you think, Bob?" Margaret asked.

"Looks straightforward enough," I said. "Nothing like the 'Dangerous Islands'!" I quipped. She flashed me a grin as we both understood. Most navigators prefer to sail around the Tuamotus, rather than negotiate their way through the scatter of islands and reefs. We had successfully visited Ahi, an island in the group, despite the fact that the word "Tuamotus" literally means "dangerous islands." After our navigational coup, we always referred to them by that name as if to magnify our private triumph.

"Okay," she answered. "Let's do it! You're the captain, captain!"

That was true. I was the captain. That made me responsible for everybody's mistakes. Especially mine.

"Okay then. We'll stay on a heading of 268 degrees, and run before the wind. We oughta make great time, Margaret!"

"This is Bravo *** Delta Zebra with the Pacific Maritime Net. The weather here in Hawaii is seventy-eight degrees with the barometer reading at twenty-nine point thirty. The skies are clear and the wind is fifteen knots out of the southeast."

"The base stations that will be checking in with us tonight are Colin, Zebra Lima *** Bravo Kilo Delta, in New Zealand and Bruce, Delta Kilo *** Delta Foxtrot, in Sydney. They'll be on with the weather in their areas toward the end of the check-in."

"Are there any Maritime Mobile Units out there that need to be priority traffic? This is Bravo *** Delta Zebra standing by with the Pacific Maritime Net..."

"This is Whiskey Romeo *** X-ray Golf with priority traffic. We're at latitude twenty-four degrees south, longitude 176 degrees west."

"The generator that powers our navigation equipment has started to give us some trouble. It's a Heber, model 730A. If possible, we'd like to talk over our problem with someone familiar with these units. Anyone out there who could give us some pointers? This is Whiskey Romeo *** X-ray Golf standing by..."

"This is Lima November *** Sierra Tango. I may be able to help you with that Heber. Let's go to 1560 and talk it over. This is Lima November *** Sierra Tango, clear with the Pacific Maritime Net."

"This is Whiskey Romeo *** X-ray Golf switching to 1560. I'll be back for check-in with you, Mac. Whiskey Romeo *** X-ray Golf clear with the Pacific Maritime Net."

"Okay. This is Bravo *** Delta Zebra with the Pacific Maritime Net. Is there any more priority traffic? Bravo *** Delta Zebra standing by..."

"All right then. Let's start the check-in. Bravo *** Delta Zebra calling Kilo Alpha *** Quebec India India."

"This is Kilo Alpha *** Quebec India India. Hi Mac, from all of us on the *Vamonos*. We're at twenty-one degrees, five minutes south latitude and 161 degrees, west longitude, first day out of Rarotonga. The winds are twenty knots out of the east and the seas are high. We're making about eight knots and the ride is smooth, Bob, Chris and I are all well. The skies are overcast though. This is Kilo Alpha *** Quebec India India standing by with the Pacific Maritime Net."

"This is Zebra Lima *** Bravo Kilo Delta in New Zealand. Hello there, Margaret. My name's Colin Busch. We haven't met on the radio before, and as you're headed down here, I thought I'd introduce myself. Zebra Lima *** Bravo Kilo Delta standing by..."

"This is Kilo Alpha *** Quebec India India. Very nice to meet you, Colin. I can't tell you what a kick we — you know, we Americans — get out of that New Zealand accent. It'll be a pleasure hearing your weather reports. Kilo Alpha *** Quebec India India standing by..."

"This is Zebra Lima *** Bravo Kilo Delta. On behalf of all my fellow Kiwis, I thank you. We get quite a kick out of you Yanks, too. Now, I guess we'd better let Mac get on with the check-in. Have a good sail, Margaret. Zebra Lima *** Bravo Kilo Delta standing by on the Pacific Maritime Net..."

FOUR

El Niño, ehl NEEN yoh, is a warm current in the Pacific Ocean that flows southward along the west coast of South America. It warms the normally cold waters off the coast of Equador and Peru. El Niño, a Spanish term meaning the child, usually occurs around Christmas, and its name refers to the Christ child.... But scientists use the term El Niño to describe a longer event with widespread effects.... A powerful El Niño in 1982 and 1983 caused severe drought in Australia and Indonesia, and an unusually large number of storms in California. It produced violent rains and destructive floods in Ecuador and Peru.

Scientists believe El Niño is related to a shift in air movements over the tropical Pacific Ocean. Changes in wind direction cause changes in the circulation and temperature of the ocean, which in turn further disrupt air movements and ocean currents.

—The World Book Encyclopedia, 1993 Edition

"When El Niño arrived, it was awesome. The Tahiti-Darwin pressure anomaly registered the strongest ever. The trade winds faltered, and the equatorial current reversed direction across the entire Pacific."

— Dr. Eugene Rasmusson, National Oceanic and Atmospheric Administration
National Geographic, February 1984

Day three out of Rarotonga
November 9, 1982
Aboard the Vamonos

The day started out leisurely. Normal shipboard routine called for us to check the rigging and forestays, and adjust the sails if the wind-direction indicator recorded a shift.

After breakfast, we had a Bible discussion. As Jehovah's Witnesses, this was an important part of our lives. After that, we would generally find a comfortable spot and do a little recreational reading. The chance to read was one of the great benefits of sailing for pleasure. The day before, Margaret had just finished reading to us from "Papillon," the survival tale of French prisoners who escaped from Devil's Island.

Even though I hadn't spoken to Chris as yet, he seemed to be more his usual happy self. Perhaps it was in spite of how he really felt, but I didn't know for sure. I would find out.

The only real cloud on our horizon that morning was literally the cloud cover itself. The great, gray expanse of clouds overhead simply would not burn off. In the South Pacific, blue skies punctuated by large, dark cloud formations are the norm. But we were now into our second straight day of overcast skies. That meant we could not take a sun shot with the sextant in order to determine our exact position.

Before the advent of satellite positioning systems, mariners relied on two basic methods to determine their position. The first, and less reliable, is called dead reckoning. By measuring your speed, direction and the elapsed time since your last known location, a rough approximation of your position can be determined. However, after several days, minor errors can add up to a major miscalculation. We had gotten as good as you can get at using dead reckoning, but it is never precise. More reliable is determining your position with the use of a sextant and timepiece. By measuring the angle of the sun above the horizon at exactly twelve o'clock noon a few calculations can fix your position with precision. If a noon sighting is not possible, then other times can be used, as well as a sunset shot or star positions at night. All sightings, however, require clear skies, and a horizon.

I knew aproximately where we were. The self steering vane had been set for 268 degrees. But wind vanes do not stay exactly on course, varying slightly in response to changes in the wind. So standing in the cockpit, I was subject to the same nagging doubts about our position that have plagued captains since time immemorial.

A few hours outside of Rarotonga, I had tried several different sail combinations. The twin genoas stretching out before the boat were designed to make maximum use of the wind. At times we had been moving along at eight knots. Ten knots was the maximum our knotmeter would measure so we were doing well. But as we went along, the wind began shifting from due west to slightly north of west. I had tried to compensate by pulling in the starboard genny and letting out the port genny sheet while adjusting the vane. But a magnetic compass can consistently read 268 degrees and the vessel remain unvaryingly headed that direction, yet be sliding slightly sideways through the water.

I told myself we were okay, but I really needed the added assurance of a reliable sextant reading. Until then, I could not be sure.

Chris was below deck reading a thriller when I called to him. "Son, I'm going to haul down the gennies. Come and help."

He jumped up without hesitation just like a good sailor. "What's the matter, Dad? We're cutting along great!" he declared.

"I know. But until I can get a shot and fix our position, I want to take it slower," I explained. I had decided to put up a storm jib since it didn't catch as much wind as the gennies did. "We better reef in the mains'l as well," I added. "Maybe we can get a good sun shot at noon."

Mid-morning Margaret fired up the radio and checked in with our little "cockroach net."

"This is Kilo Alpha *** Quebec India India, calling Hotel Charlie *** Foxtrot Bravo Charlie. I repeat, this is Kilo Alpha *** Quebec India India, calling Hotel Charlie *** Foxtrot Bravo Charlie. Kilo Alpha *** Quebec India India standing by..."

"This is Hotel Charlie *** Foxtrot Bravo Charlie calling Kilo Alpha *** Quebec India India. Good morning, Margaret. How're you all doing out there? Mary and I left Rarotonga this morning along with Dave and Jan on the *Karana*. We've been underway about three hours now. The seas are high but we're getting plenty of wind."

"I can still see the *Karana* off the stern, so Dave and Jan are moving along pretty well themselves."

"Margaret, what's your position and what's the weather like out there? This is Hotel Charlie *** Foxtrot Bravo

Charlie standing by."

"This is Kilo Alpha *** Quebec India India. Good to hear your voice, Tom. The seas are a bit high here too but, same as for you, the wind is strong. Blowing at about twenty knots out of the east. We figure our position at twenty-one degrees south latitude, one hundred sixty-seven degrees west longitude. We haven't been able to get a good fix because of the overcast, but we hope to get one today. We're having a good sail, though. Dave, are you out there? This is Kilo Alpha *** Quebec India India standing by."

"This is Tango Tango *** Lima Bravo Echo. Margaret and Bob and Chris, too, hi to you all. We heard your broadcast to Tom and Mary and it sounds like you're doing well."

"We can still see Tom and Mary on the horizon but the distance is growing."

"It'll be good to hear from you as we go along. Margaret, we got some nice pictures of the *Vamonos* from Rarotonga. We'll show them to you when we catch up to you in New Zealand. This is Tango Tango *** Lima Bravo Echo standing by."

"This is Kilo Alpha *** Quebec India India. Sounds like we're all doing well. Have either of you caught any fish, or seen any, since you've been out? It hasn't been very long, I know. I'm just asking. We haven't seen fish in three days, now. This is Kilo Alpha *** Quebec India India standing by."

"This is Tango Tango *** Lima Bravo Echo. Well no, we haven't seen any. Our lines are out and I saw Mary, up ahead, put one out a couple of hours ago and it's still there. That's a little peculiar, isn't it?"

"In any case, I still haven't given my position. It's twenty-one degrees south..."

Soon after 11:30, Margaret and I began our drill for the noon sun shot. Also, if the sun peeked out at, say, a quarter of, we'd shoot it then. If we could get a shot before noon, then wait until the sun transited the zenith and got to the same sextant altitude again on its way "down", we could do some simple subtraction and find the exact time of the zenith; obviously, the sun's not directly overhead at exactly noon everywhere in the time zone. From there, the nautical calculations are greatly simplified. That's called using T1 and T2, "T" meaning Time. But if necessary, getting just one altitude with its exact time would be enough. The navigation references we'd calculate with are very complicated. One altitude would just mean more working through the books and more calculations. The noon shot, with its T1 and T2, was simpler so we preferred it.

Even with reduced speed, we were rocking pretty vigorously, and sighting through a sextant requires as much stability as possible. I was amidships at first, with Margaret across the beam from me.

"Bob, what time do you have?"

"Uh... eleven-thirty four on my mark... now."

"Good. That's what I have. These quartz watches are great." To be sure, you often check your timepiece with a radio source, in our case the National Bureau of Standards broadcast from Kauai, but our watches had little error.

"Yep. Boy, this is so rocky. I'm going to have an awful time if the seas don't calm." I was sighting through a Weems and Plath Micrometer Drum sextant whose mirrors — you don't want to be looking directly at the sun — are optical quality, and which is accurate to angles corresponding to a two inch width over a distance of one nautical mile. A nautical mile is a little longer than a statute land mile. One point one five statute miles, to be exact.

This beauty — German-built cast brass with a satin finish, adjustable handle for comfort, battery-powered lights for nighttime noting of degrees of arc and on the micrometer area — cost about a thousand dollars. But you have to have an accurate sextant. Plastic sextants, like the emergency one stowed in the dinghies, were better than nothing, but not nearly so good as this.

"Margaret, let's move a bit aft. Maybe I can steady myself against the cabin. With all this wind, the seas are so high... This is gonna be some trick. No, this isn't much better..."

Chris always watched the sightings. It is, after all, one of the things most fun about being a sailor. And to a seventeen year old, fun was important. Truth be told, it was fun for me, too.

Except now, when I was worried about our position and was navigating, so to speak, in the dark.

"Dad," he said. "Try the lazaret deck. You might as well get as far aft as you can."

It was a good idea, the stern being the boat's most stable area, made better by the fact that I could also balance myself against the stanchions there. Once braced, I looked through the glass and could see the bit of glare that was the sun, now fronted by thinner clouds. Quickly I started adjusting the instrument's arc to get the horizon lined up in the other mirror.

"What time is it, Margaret?"

"Eleven-forty three."

"Pretty glarey, Dad."

"I know, but it's something. If I can just get it ri... Mark!"

"Right!" said Margaret instantly, starting to write down the hour, minute, and second, but I said, "No, not good..."

The rocking! And the fact, of course, that the sun was not a solid object in the glass but a wash of white.

"Mark! No... M... I can't... Mark! Not good..."

This went on. In spite of the fresh wind, I was sweating. It was very long, that seventeen minutes. Then it was noon. Then noon was past.

Could I move somewhere else? I wanted that to be an option, a solution. But it wasn't; I was on the stablest part of the boat. Concentrate, Bob. The moment comes, it does come, although it passes quickly. You just have to catch it.

The sun broke through. A clear orb, swinging through a corner of the darkened glass. I adjusted. I almost said "mark", I still had to get the moment...

"Mark! Wait — well, write it down. But I can get it better..."

The sea seemed suddenly to be acting up even more. Was it trying to stop me from getting the shot? Don't be stupid. Concentrate.

"Mm... wait... m... mark!"

When I didn't retract it, Margaret quickly wrote down the time. She told me later she was sure she had noted the second correctly; she'd been using the stopwatch function on her watch. For my part, it was not a completely right mark, the alignment had just passed, but it was close. It should do fine.

"What time is it, Margaret?"

"Twelve-fourteen, now."

"Twelve-fourteen! How could it be twelve-fourteen already!"

"Don't yell at me, Bob. It's twelve-fourteen!"

"Right, right. Sorry. Well, that should be all right..."

"Calculate it, right?"

"Yes. Go ahead. Sorry about yelling."

"Oh, that's all right. It must have been frustrating."

"Yeah, you did good, Dad. Real good."

"Thanks," I said.

Half an hour later, Margaret came back on deck with the finished calculations. She said, "Well, we're farther north, all right. Twenty degrees and ten minutes South latitude, 166 degrees and fifty minutes West longitude."

"What?! Oh, boy, so far north... And 166 degrees and fifty minutes west longitude? That far west already? That's incredible." Why were the wind and current moving so contrary to form? Instead of the usual south-westerly direction, they'd actually moved us west-northwest, and very quickly.

I went below into the main salon and looked over our chart. These nautical charts are much more involved than a regular map. They have depth readings dotted all over the stretches of ocean, for instance. They have the names of narrow passages between islands. They also show whatever tiny reefs have been reported, and indicate roughly, their size.

This section of chart showed me that we were somewhat north and east of Haran Reef, with Beveridge Reef west of us. I plotted a new course that would take us southwest, passing south of Beveridge and then Haran on our port side. Before, I'd figured to pass below them, but now we were too far west for that. The chance of hitting one of these tiny specks in the vast expanse of the ocean was remote, but I eyed them carefully anyway.

On a course of 234 degrees we'd pass those two, then an even smaller speck which had no name, then we'd be in open sea all the way to the Kermadec Islands. We'd pass north of these, the way I'd wanted to anyway, and head on to New Zealand. I logged the plot underneath Margaret's entry of the sighting and position, then stopped and thought that perhaps I should change to 235 degrees, give it a little more leeway to pass the reefs. No, that's ridiculous — a degree translated into a width of sixty nautical miles on the chart projection, and we were talking about a couple of formations maybe a hundred feet across each. The chance of hitting one was astronomical, now that I thought of it. Besides, the current running west would probably clear us even more than my line plot showed. I went above decks to change our course.

Chris and Margaret were there waiting, knowing we'd be adjusting the sails. In this case we'd be sheeting in, turning with the wind behind us. Taking my position in the cockpit, I looked over to Chris and Margaret, he seated on the starboard side, she on the port.

I said, "Stand by to change course." They had already checked for and stowed loose gear. Now they uncleated the sheets. I unlocked the wheel.

"Ready," said Chris, who was farthest from the mains'l and boom.

"Ready," said Margaret.

"Changing course!" I called, turning the wheel. Margaret quickly trimmed the main sheet and, in the fresh wind, the boom tightened up briskly. Now with the mainsail hauled in close we were listing hard to starboard. We'd remain that way for a while, so Margaret went below to secure a few things. I was glad they had got so good at working the sails. The greatest hazard on a sailboat is a moving boom.

"Well done, guys!" I yelled. Now we were on a heading of 234 degrees and, if my sighting proved accurate, we could stay on it pretty much all the way to the Kermedecs. When the overcast broke again, I'd try to get another sun shot or a dusk starshot.

Suddenly, the ringer attached to one of the fishing lines clanged. We had a strike. Although we hadn't had a nibble in the three days out, we had something now, and from the look of the line, something big.

"Chris! Strike on the line! Loosen up on the jib and lower the mains'l!"

"Wow, great!" he yelled, scrambling. We had the *Vamonos*'s power slacked in about three minutes, and we began winching in the line. The fish was fighting with a lot of strength, a lot of weight. I cranked the winch for maybe three or four minutes, then Chris spelled me. I had just taken it back when the fish rushed toward the surface. I winched like crazy. We saw its green and yellow color and it seemed about five feet long. Chris grabbed the trophy glove and, when the fish was close enough, started to haul it, hand over hand, out of the sea.

"It's a mahi-mahi," I said.

"No..," grunted Chris.

"Yes," Margaret said. "It's a mahi-mahi."

"No!" he yelled, but said no more until he had shipped the fish. Breathing hard, he said, "No. Look at it. A mahi-mahi has a square head. From profile. This has a longer, thinner head. It's a wahoo."

"It is?" said Margaret.

"Yes!"

"Chris, don't talk like that to her."

He didn't answer me. He went below. I'd have to talk to him. The tension between them, and between me and him as a result, was likely to make the whole sail unpleasant. Certainly, it could spoil what would have been a happy feast on this fish and our fresh fruit.

It was nine p.m. and Margaret was on the radio with the Pacific Maritime Net. She was the one with the license and, it's interesting: Even though I was the captain of the *Vamonos*, they had to know that Margaret was on board before they would receive my transmission. Once, I'd innocently called in with our call-sign and the base station had said, "Uh, who's this?" "Bob Aros," I'd said, "on the *Vamonos*." "Well, uh, where's Margaret?" they'd said. "Coming down the ladder right now." So they'd said, "Well, put her on." Once Margaret had identified herself, they'd been willing to accept a transmission from me.

"This is Kilo Alpha *** Quebec India India," she was saying. "We've changed course. We took a noon shot which put our position at twenty degrees ten minutes south latitude, 166 degrees fifty minutes west longitude. So we changed course to 234 degrees. That put us on a broad reach and besides that, the weather has become a lot worse, so we're having a rough ride. The wind's at thirty knots out of the east-southeast and it's kicking up the waves good and high. It's got us riding at about a twenty-five degree angle. We reefed our sails around sundown but it's still, well, it's a rough ride."

I was getting drowsy. Margaret had outdone herself with dinner and I was overfull: wahoo steak with butter and garlic, papaya slices, sliced bananas in cream sauce, mango slices dripping juice. We'd washed the feast down with beer and also some of the orange juice we'd squeezed the day before. We'd got four quarts of wonderful juice and still had bags of oranges left. After we'd given away all that fruit to Tom and Mary and Dave and Jan, we still had over a hundred pounds of it in the forward "V" berth. So much that I slept instead in the main salon on the dinette berth. A hundred pounds of fruit for three people on a two week trip was around seventeen pounds per week each. Too much to finish.

"...So, Margaret," the Hawaii base station was saying, "it's rough there but you have it under control, is that right? Bravo *** Delta Zebra standing by..."

"This is Kilo Alpha *** Quebec India India. That's about it, Mac, and maybe the weather will calm during the night. That's all for us here. Goodnight, Mac. Kilo Alpha *** Quebec India India clear with the Pacific Maritime Net."

"This is Bravo *** Delta Zebra. Our base operator in New Zealand, Colin Busch, wasn't on the net tonight and won't be tomorrow night either, because he's visiting friends. So let's get the New Zealand weather from the friend he got to sit in for him. Are you out there, Victor November *** Sierra Golf Romeo...?"

"Let's set the watches," I said. "Margaret, will you go first? If you take nine to twelve, you can wake me at midnight."

"Fine," she said.

"Okay," Chris said. "I'm wiped out." And he went off to sleep in the quarter-berth. I headed for the dinette berth, really just a seat cushion covering the main food supplies stowed in the seat. Margaret would replace me there when her watch was over.

About ten o'clock, I was awakened from a sound sleep

when some books fell on my head from the shelves above me.
"Are you two alright down there?" came Margaret's
concerned call from topside.
"Chris?" I called out.
"I'm alright!" he called back. "What happened?"
Margaret answered, "A rogue wave. There's some sea
out there."
"Are we still on course?" I asked thickly.
"Yes. But, you know, Bob, with this broad reach, the boat
is really crashing through the water. We must be listing
twenty-five degrees to starboard." she declared. "Every
once in a while, a wave will crash into the hull. I'm afraid
to move from the cockpit to the deck. I could get swept
away out there. The wind's at twenty or thirty knots. Why
is it blowing so hard at night?" she asked.
"It's alright. Everything's fine. Just read your book.
We'll be all right." I tried to assure her.
"You know, I try to read, but every two or three minutes I
look up for lights. I can't seem to relax. I get afraid. It's
like the Matterhorn ride at Disneyland up here. My
adrenaline's pumping. " She yelled back.
"I know, I know," It's just some weather. We'll be fine."
I declared confidently. "Wake me at midnight."
She accepted my answer but was still apprehensive as I
rolled over and tried to get back to sleep. I rehearsed all the
reasons I could think of for believing my own advice. The
boat was seaworthy. We were on course. The weather
wasn't that bad. It was just a little rougher than we liked it.
But everything would be just fine. A little adventure will
make for good tales when we get to New Zealand. It is just
like Disneyland. A little excitement, a little feeling of
danger, but in the end everything turns out safe and secure.
Safe and secure...I smiled as we leaned hard to starboard.
Everything's going to be just fine...

FIVE

"The entire reef is underwater at high tide. Only at low water do a very few pieces of coral break the surface. In other words, there is nothing normally above water most of the time to indicate the presence of Beveridge Reef."
— Don McClead, Associate Member, Seven Seas Cruising Association
Commodore's Bulletin, October, 1983

End of Day three out of Rarotonga
November 9, 1982
Aboard the Vamonos

"We've hit a reef, Chris! We've hit a reef!" But before he could ask another question for which I did not have an answer, I turned back to Margaret, still staring over the side in shock.

"C'mon, Margaret! C'mon! I need you!" I yelled.

She turned back to me, and I saw some life return to her eyes.
"Quick! Get on the radio! Get out a Mayday!"
She nodded thickly, and headed below.
I reached into the lazaret and started to pull on my wet suit. "Maybe she's not too badly breached," I said to Chris.
"Dad, let's try to anchor her." he offered.
"Yes!" I snapped back in agreement.
He ran to the forward pulpit, released the windlass, and the anchor paid out immediately onto the reef. It was a C.Q.R. anchor, excellent for penetration in weeds, coral, mud. Chris ran back toward me through the howling wind. The sea threw another wave, moving the boat farther along. In the dim light we saw the anchor sweep back past us, washed beyond the boat.
"It didn't catch," I said. "Let's get the stern anchor out."
As I released it, Chris said, "I should go down with it and secure it."
Margaret screamed, "No!!" from the cockpit behind us. I turned to see her on the companionway ladder. "Not without a lifejacket!"
"Right. You're right," I said, and she darted below decks. Chris and I got our tennis shoes, went back on deck, and put them on. Margaret reappeared with two jackets. She looked much paler than she had the moment before.
"What is it?" I asked, struggling into mine.
"It's nothing, only... when I went into the 'V' berth, there was no light and I didn't want to turn anything on. Do you smell the gas? And I had to shut the door behind me to get at the locker... I thought if we went off the reef while I was in there, it'd take me down, trapped in the bow — in the dark."
"Oh honey... All right. We'll get out of this. Get your life jacket on." And then softly, "You get some things together.

Food and things."

A wave hit the boat and almost knocked me off my feet.

"Okay, Chris, go ahead. Carefully — hold onto the chain." I paid out some of it as he swung over the side. The anchor reached the reef, the chain slackened, he grabbed it and lowered himself down. Picking up the anchor, he steadied himself just before a wave hit him. He kept his feet.

This one was a performance anchor. With its long, sharp flukes, it was great for mud and sand, but has limited penetration. Still, a ridge or outcropping would hold it just fine. Chris started walking it out, feeling with his soles in about three feet of water. Another wave hit him, knocked him down, and he sat for a second, spluttering. "Kind of rough out here," he shouted. Getting up, he started out again, waves hitting him about ten seconds apart. He'd brace for the bigger ones, but some knocked him down anyway.

"Dad, it's smooth! It's brain-coral!"

"All right. I'm coming down, too," I yelled over the roar of the surf, the singing of parted lines in the wind. He had several yards of the chain played out to him, so I secured the windlass and stepped over the side, lowering myself on the slippery chain. Almost at the bottom, I waited while a big wave broke against the hull, pushing it back across the reef, swinging me, then I dropped into the three feet of water. How wide was the reef? How long before the sea pushed it over the edge?

"I'll use the bow anchor," I shouted, starting to make my way out to where it lolled in the roiling surf. I thought, "If the moon will just stay out..." and as I did, the clouds hid it. I kept going, waves hitting and rushing past, ramming the boat, pushing it screeching over the surface. The moon reappeared. I got to the C.Q.R. and hefted its thirty-five pounds. I was about at the center of the *Vamonos*, Christian six feet to my right. I'd been feeling with my feet as I made my way out. The surface was mildly abrasive — no deep pits, no jagged outcroppings. For all intents and purposes, or at least our purposes, it was smooth.

I bent my knees as a wave crashed into me. "Let's both go straight out," I called over the din.

"Okay, Dad. Try keeping your legs bent all the time."

"Okay," I shouted. Skating my feet, I pulled the anchor on its chain, the waves along its length jerking it as they hit. The air was full of the smell of saltwater, the taste of it. There must be something down here, I thought. Something to anchor to. Something to save the boat.

The moon peek-a-booed in and then back out, giving a beautiful silver lining to the clouds. I could see well at those times. I reached forward with one foot and a wave hit me and pushed me back, falling. As I stood up, another hit me and drove me farther back, rolling me around. As I got to my knees I turned to the *Vamonos*.

The ripped, flapping sails cracked like pistol shots, silvery in the moonlight. The severed lines waved everywhere madly in the wind. Spray shot up past the deck as waves hit the hull. And the hull... was split open from bow to stern. Light streamed out from the interior, split above full-length split. The tongue-and-groove strips of mahogany that made up the hull had torqued apart. It was as if some giant beast had ripped its talons along the underbelly, leaving it to die on Beveridge Reef.

I picked myself up, cradling the C.Q.R, and turned toward the sea. Chris was on his butt, only four feet ahead of me, having been knocked back by another wave. "Anything there?" I called hoarsely.

"There was something, just a second ago," he gasped. "I think I felt a hole but then a wave got me."

"Try to find it again."

"Yeah, that's what I was gonna do."

He got to his feet and we both struggled forward, staying pretty close, staying centered on the boat in case we got knocked all the way back. If we did, the hull would keep us from being swept away.

A hollow "Boom!" came from behind us as a vast wave hammered the crippled sloop. Spray splashed into my eyes, stinging, as I yanked on the chain and felt my way forward. Nothing. Smooth.

This went on in the shrieking, pounding night, intermittently bright and then black as the moon and clouds played their game. The sails cracked, the lines sang. Our home screeched behind us, the chains pulling us back when at times we reached their limits, each wave pushing the ship across the width of the reef. How much more did it have before it fell into the deep, pulling us all with it? Smooth, so smooth.

A wave hit me and knocked me back, then another churned around me, sweeping me back. As I was rising, a third one flung me back and my head cracked into the hull. I pushed forward to my knees and Chris came twisting in a breaking wave and slammed into the boat five feet from me.

"Bob!!" Margaret's voice through the split hull was surprising, shocking.

"We're all right!" I yelled. "Son," I called over the roar, "are you okay?"

"Yeah!" he shouted back. "Dad, I can't get it. Can't find anything for the anchor."

Now there was a new smell out on the reef. Gasoline. The fuel lines had ruptured. "No holes at all out there?"

"Nothing," he said.

"I don't know how long the boat can last."

"Yeah. Looks like it's in deeper water."

We stood up and started to push our way out again.

"No," I said, halting. "We'd better stop." Chris looked at me. I turned to the *Vamonos*. "We'd better get ready to abandon ship."

Chris had regained the deck and I followed up the stern anchor chain, my handholds slipping, arms already weary from hauling the useless C.Q.R. I got my head to deck level and shouted to him, "Go get what you need." He dove down the companionway.

I followed him, calling, "Margaret! We have to go."

She was forward, just aft of the "V" berth door, getting the chart from its rack. Something bumped into my knee and I looked down stupidly to see the navigation desk I'd hand-crafted from fine oak floating in three feet of water. Books floated there too, and our clothes, and other parts of our lives. Directly in front of me was the four inch thick dinette pole, a structural brace running from floor to ceiling. The torque had torn it in half; it was dangling foolishly.

The water was rising quickly now. Margaret turned, said, "I took food. I have our passports, the chart, the nautical books, the compass, the Bible — ohh, the pages are so thin, they're ruined from the water — I'll take the *Yearbook*. It's got the daily Scripture readings in it."

"Great, Margaret. Real good. We've got to go. The boat's full of fumes. The lights are still on in here, the batteries are on —"

"I know. They could spark. I'm scared to death."

"We've got to break out the dinghies." I turned aft to where Chris was hoisting a canvas bag. "Come on. Come on, son," I said.

Topside, the hard dinghy was lashed to the cabin roof. In it were supplies and the deflated rubber dinghy. Chris and I unlashed the hard dinghy, hauled it down, and unloaded it to get at the inflatable. Also its foot pump. Another big wave skidded the sloop across the reef with a shriek. How much more room did it have? How much? One more wave?

Chris started to inflate the rubber dinghy, a one-man job, and I looked aft and saw our bag of ripe coconuts. I rushed to it and, with the knife from the lazaret, I cut it away from the stern stanchions. Food and water together in about twenty green containers. I hoisted the bag to my chest, turned, and the sack split open, spilling the coconuts into the sea. My mouth fell open.

Margaret was on deck, now, wrestling with the hard dinghy. I joined her and quickly secured its painter to the boat's railing. We heaved it into the water. I saw the soft dinghy sail over the rail as Chris flung it past me. He tied off its painter and said, "What else, Dad?"

I wanted every little vessel we could get. I said, "Get the windsurfer," and he rushed to do it.

Reaching down to the deck, I picked up the spare sextant and the first-aid kit which we'd tumbled out of the hard dinghy to get at the inflatable. I threw them into the rubber dinghy as it swelled up off the reef next to the *Vamonos*. Margaret threw in a stuffed, bulky pillowcase, tied at its mouth. I grabbed Chris's bag from the deck and heaved it in. We could see the water rising around us.

Margaret picked up the ten pound bag of fresh oranges that had been in the hard dinghy, threw them — and missed. The dinghy had lurched just as she heaved the bag. The bag was gone instantly.

"Ohhh!" she said.

"We've got to get off!" I yelled. Chris was back. "Jump in the soft dinghy and pull the surfer over," I shouted to him. Its tough bottom took his weight easily. The wind howled. I took a duffel bag that Margaret had brought up and threw it to him. He stowed it. "Lash the surfer on, too. Jump, Margaret!"

"Bob..."

"You gotta jump, Margaret!"

She jumped, and I followed. We tied the dinghies together on a short line and let go the painters from the railing. Instantly we were swept past the *Vamonos*. Her tall sails were trailing in the water, billowing crazily in the banshee wind. Her cabin house was lurched over and under water. The mast was at a forty-five degree angle.

Then we were gone and the blackness surrounded us.

A heartbeat later, I thought, Maybe I could have put a thirty-foot line on her, moored us to her. Maybe there's a lagoon here. But no! It could explode! And even if it didn't, maybe it was 2000 feet deep here and the line would pull us down with the sloop. Maybe the suction as she went under would still pull us down. But if only we could have anchored her, we would have had time to get whatever we wanted, get all the food there was, take the best clothes for the situation. We'd have had time to think! If she hadn't exploded.

Margaret said, in a low voice, "At least we're all

together."

Yes, we were together, but going where? The clouds broke a little, exposing the almost full moon.

Then I heard Chris, from the other dinghy: "I see bottom!"

Margaret and I looked. "I don't see anything."

"Neither do I."

I didn't want to see anything. That would have meant that I should have tied on with the thirty-foot line. It would mean we were in a lagoon.

Minutes passed. "I see bottom again!"

We looked down and, three feet below us, there was coral! I thought if it got any higher it would rip open the inflatable. Suddenly we were on another reef... No, the same reef! It's a circular reef! I thought. With a lagoon in the middle! Can we? No, of course no anchors in a dinghy — Could we jump out? Let the dinghies go? Not with the supplies — Could I jump out and hold the two dinghies back? — And that second we were over the other side and into the sea.

The swells rose right away, up and up as we swept into open sea, ten feet, up again, fifteen feet, the wind catching crests and showering us with spray. The clouds closed again.

No one spoke for awhile. Then Chris's voice came across the stretch, "It'll be all right. We'll be all right."

"Yes, son," I said.

"That's right," said Margaret.

"I'm gonna sleep," said Chris.

"Is it wet in there, Chris?" asked Margaret.

"Yeah, but it's okay."

We said good night.

Margaret and I lay back in the Sandpiper. It was wet and cold. The three of us had down jackets on, which helped.

We would have been wetter and colder without them. But it was still wet and cold. I tried to calmly let what had happened sink in. I couldn't get calm. I began worrying because the dinghies bumped into each other constantly. If that kept up, the Avon might puncture.

I pulled over one of the oars and handed it to Margaret. "Here, hold this."

"What for?"

"We're gonna make a sail."

I took the windsurfer sail out of its bag that was laying in the Sandpiper. I tied the dacron bag around my wife's oar and then around the second oar I was holding. We held it up and it caught the wind.

"Is this going to help us go faster?" she asked.

"That's not the point," I said. "It's just to separate us from the Avon a little. I'm afraid if they rub, it'll puncture. Margaret... I'm so sorry. I'm..." And I choked.

"It's not your fault. I'm the one that's sorry, I was on watch. It was my fault."

"No, it is my fault. I took the shot, I set the course... I yelled at you when we were taking the shot — I'm sorry for that, too. I'm sorry for it all."

We wept and hugged each other. We prayed.

We held the little sail up for about an hour. Our arms couldn't take more than that. We let it down.

SIX

"We have a Tuita navigator proverb that says, `It is enough to strike the row of puko trees. You need not hit a particular tree. In the same way, a canoe captain would aim for the middle of the group, instead of for an individual island."

—Ve'ehala, governor of Ha'apai. *National Geographic*, December 1974

Day one in the dinghies
November 10, 1982
Dawn

My body ached. When I thought of our situation, my mind ached, too.

The swells were down to five feet, coursing us up and

down like a roller-coaster ride that just didn't stop. The waves came from behind us, lifting us, cresting and going past, dropping us down its back side into the trough, where another one was waiting to take over, lifting us yet again. And again. And again.

They struck no fear in me. Not then.

Margaret stirred next to me, and I called toward the soft dinghy, "Chris. Wake up." He roused himself sleepily, looked around, and actually grinned at me.

"Well, here we are, Dad."

"Yes. So. Let's get organized."

The Sandpiper, our hard dinghy, had been tugging, then scraping, at the rubber dinghy all night. I was afraid the line between them would rip through the loop hole of the softer craft.

"Let's try lashing the dinghies side by side." The soft dinghy rode slightly behind us, its bow tied to our stern with the five foot line. I threw Chris a fifteen foot line, saying, "Tie that to your bow," while I passed it through our own bow loop. Hauling on it, I gradually brought the two dinghies side by side. Chris undid the shorter line from his bow, passed it through his stern loop, and used it to pull our dinghy's stern next to his, finally tying it off. I paddled us reasonably straight before the following waves and said, "We'll see how that works."

Chris asked, "What next, Dad?" He was downright chipper. Kids.

"Let's take stock."

I asked Margaret for the chart. "Okay, we could have gone down on Beveridge Reef, or farther southwest on Haran Reef. We'll take a sunshot and be sure. But in any case, we know the current was strong west-northwest. Drifting with the current, I make our speed to be one to two knots, so let's figure one and a half... at that rate, going steady west-northwest, say 285 degrees, we're headed for... the Tongan Islands. Well, that's not too bad. Plenty of islands in that group. Yes, I'll plot it, but that looks about right."

"We might get picked up way before that, Dad. A day or two."

"Yeah, we might, but you know there's not much commercial traffic out this way. Few flights, which'd be much too high, anyway, and not many liners. No commercial shipping lanes at all. But there's always a chance."

"Sure. We sent out a Mayday. They'll be looking for us."

"No, we didn't send out a Mayday," Margaret said. "When I went below, I fired up the radio right away. The lights came on but right away they died. Water had got to it. It was dead."

"Dead?! How could that be?"

I cut in, "Chris, the boat went aground at a forty-five degree angle."

"That stinks," he scowled. "That stinks..." Then his face brightened. "But, oh well, come ten o'clock, they'll miss us on the cockroach net."

"That's right," Margaret said. "And at nine-thirty tonight, we won't make our other check-in on the Maritime Net."

I said, "Okay, but assuming the worst, I think we can make Tonga in seven or eight, maybe nine days. Yeah, say seven to nine days. Let's treat this like we're on just another sea voyage and Tonga is our next port of call."

"Right," said Chris, with that inexplicable cheeriness. "Off to Tonga. What now, Dad?"

"Let's see what we have, the supplies," I said, reaching

for the duffel bag. I already had checked that the usual survival items were still in the dinghy where we had stowed them: the sewing kit with sail needles and sail thread, the small first-aid kit with antibiotics, the emergency sextant, three oars, a flare gun and some parachute flares, flashlight, fishing tackle, and what's called a solar still, for precipitating fresh water from sea water. We had a bag of rope from the lazaret which I must have pulled out at some point. Chris's bag was full of shirts and pants and he had his survival knife. I had my dive knife, but only the wet suit in the way of clothes. There were three life preservers, the kind that slip over your head, and a cushion life preserver. Also the five-gallon can of water, and Margaret had thrown four or five liter bottles of 'Eau Royale', an early Tahitian version of designer water, into the soft dinghy.

She'd packed the main first aid supplies, the chart, the Sight Reduction Tables, our Yearbook, a plastic pouch with our passports and ship's papers, some dried food, and about ten snack packs of peanuts.

"Where's the Nautical Almanac? Where's the compass?" I asked.

Margaret's jaw dropped, then she and Chris started sifting through the duffel bag articles spread on the floor of the dinghy. They weren't there. When she looked up at me, I picked up the HO-249.

I screamed, "What good is this?!! What good is the sextant?! I can't plot a position without the Almanac or the compass! This is worthless!" And I threw the Sight Reduction Tables into the water coursing past.

"Chris and I were out there trying to save the boat!" I went on. "You were supposed to get the supplies! Don't you know how important this is?"

"I'm sorry. I took them down. I know I did. I must have laid them on the floor of the cockpit before I put them into the bag and then..."

"Are you stupid?!"

"Don't call me *stupid*! If I did a stupid thing, then all right! But don't you call me stupid!"

That caught me up short, then I went on. "Couldn't you have taken the time to do it right?"

"Bob, I thought the boat was going to slide off the reef — carry me down — It could have exploded any minute."

I was still angry. The sextant was useless. There was no way I could know where we were. The day before I must have taken a poor sighting, and I had hit a tiny reef in the vast Pacific. Now I couldn't take another shot and might miss an island in the Tongan Group. Tonga was my plan for *saving* us.

If I were a better navigator, I could have made some use of the sextant. I knew that. Joshua Slocum circumnavigated the world with a one-handed clock! But I only knew what I knew. And that wasn't enough.

I sulked. I sulked, but I shut up. Eventually it passed. I loved her, after all.

The total water content must be kept within fairly narrow limits for healthy functioning of the cells and tissues.

The concentration in the body's fluids of mineral salts and other dissolved substances also must be kept within a narrow range. In many cases of dehydration, salt will have been lost as well as water.

— American Medical Association Encyclopedia of Medicine

"Look, if we figure our position as starting from Haran Reef, I think that will be safer, because, here you can see — can you both see from there? — that if we went down on Beveridge and the current carries us west-northwest, we don't have much to worry about. We'll go right into the middle of Tonga, more or less. But if it was Haran and we're going west-northwest, there's a chance we could still pass south of the islands. Then the next landfall would be Australia, 2500 miles. That'd have to take about fifty-five days — we'd never make it. So, why I'm saying this is, if we rig an oar to act as a rudder and keep headed as much to starboard as possible, then even if it was Haran, we'd still get north enough to hit Tonga."

"Sounds good, Captain," said Chris. "What do you think, Margaret?" Chris was in a very expansive mood. He's a naturally cheery kid, but I wondered if he was also trying to make Margaret feel better after my outburst.

"Yes, that makes sense," she said. "So we'll use the oar as a rudder. Now how about the food," said Chris. "Lets eat. I'm starving."

"Great idea," I said as I picked up the pillowcase and

unknotted the end. "Let's see what we have..." I started to sort through the contents. It was mostly cans.

"They don't have any labels," said Chris.

"They're in here, they washed off," I said. I had about ten cans on the floor of the dinghy by now. Was there nothing else but cans? And how were we going to open them?

"How are we going to get them open?" asked Chris anxiously.

"Guys. There's a can opener in there," said Margaret.

"Oh. Yes, here it is," I said with relief. But then I looked up at her. "Nothing else but these, Margaret? No fruit? What about the orange juice we squeezed? Is that somewhere?"

"No, I didn't get that." She didn't sound happy.

"All those bananas in the 'V' berth?" Chris asked. "The avocados, the papayas — the honey?"

"No. I didn't think of them. The 'V' berth... I went there for the lifejackets. It was so dark... All I could think of was that we might go over the edge any second, I had to get out of there. The salon was where I cooked. That's where I went for food."

Fighting down frustration and new anger, I said slowly, "Okay. Okay... We have, uh, seventeen cans of food." I sighed. "And four, eight, ten packs of peanuts and... four packages of dried food, tuna with noodles and such. Seven to nine days to Tonga but we'd better be safe: one can of food between us every morning. For an evening meal, the peanuts — a pack a day, six or seven nuts each, will last ten days — then the dried food."

Chris said, "We can live on that."

"Yes," said Margaret. "In survival class they said you

could go a long time without food, as long as you had water."

"Let's eat," Chris said.

I put all but one can back into the pillowcase. I had no idea what this labelless can contained. It happens that fruit-cocktail is my favorite canned food. It happened that this was fruit-cocktail.

"Great," Chris said.

We bowed our heads and I said a prayer. I thanked God for the food the same way I usually did, but then I asked Him, strenuously, to help us get through this, if that was what He wanted. Then I gave thanks that we still had our lives.

I handed Chris the can, saying, "One-third of the fruit, then sip some of the juice in there." I watched him closely, not knowing how he was at judging thirds. Kids, you know. But I felt a lot calmer for having prayed.

From what I could see, the boy handed over pretty exactly two-thirds to Margaret. She ate hers quietly, using the bent lid for a scoop, as Chris had, then handed the can to me. It was good. It was very, very good.

"Okay," I said. "Let's use the can for the water. We'll fill it and have a third each. Margaret, hand me the — No, Chris, better get those liter bottles, and we'll keep them together with the big can." Chris rummaged under his pile of clothes and had started to gather the bottles when he looked up at me with a stricken expression.

"Dad, these bottles aren't full anymore." He lifted two, and I could see they had a crushed look to them. "I must have... I guess I rolled over on them in my sleep. Looks like some of the water... seeped out."

Would nothing go right? Wasn't there anything I could count on?

"Bring them over here." My voice sounded sluggish to

me. Mustn't sound like that. They counted on me to be positive. "Wait," I said. "Hand them over two at a time. Let's not lose anything." Chris kneeled in the Avon and handed them over. Each was maybe half full.

"I was so tired, Dad, I fell right asleep — I know I didn't start out on the bottles. I must have rolled over."

"All right, all right." I didn't sound as charitable as I might have.

"Margaret, let me have the five gallon jug. Let's see how much is in it." That can, hard, red plastic, looked like the ones on the back of jeeps. I opened it up and looked in at a lot more space than I expected. "It's not full," I said.

No one said anything more as I began to pour the remains of the liter bottles into the bigger jug. It became close to full. I'd thought we had the full five gallons, plus the four liters — more than a gallon more. We had about four and a half gallons.

"Okay," I broke the silence. "These food cans are sixteen ounces, same as a pint. Say we share two cans a day, two pints a day. Eight pints in a gallon, so a gallon would get us through four days. That way, this would last us about eighteen days."

Margaret said, "Well, we're figuring about half that to Tonga."

"Yeah," I said. "But if we miss Tonga? Or even coast right through the group? There are some good distances separating the islands. I think we have to play it safe. Two cans a day. That'll give us between ten and eleven ounces a day, each. Not much, but we can survive on that."

"The dinghies are seaworthy," I continued. "This Sandpiper can't sink — you could fill it with water and it wouldn't sink." Sandpipers have foam sandwiched into their bottoms and sides. For its part, the soft dinghy was not the fifty-nine dollars and ninty-five cents number one might buy from a sporting goods store, either. The Avon Redcrest is a 700 pound-capacity craft. "We have water. We have food. We have three oars, and we can use one for a rudder. We're okay. We'll be fine. We'll get through this." I felt brave that day.

I set Chris to bailing out the Avon with the empty fruit can. During the night, both the dinghies had taken on water. Just before he got started, crouching in the soft dinghy, he took something out of his shirt pocket and looked at it. A piece of cardboard, a picture, maybe? He replaced it and got to work.

Margaret and I started stowing the gear, such as it was, in the hard dinghy, neatening the area. I noticed her looking at me with a small smile. "What?" I asked.

"I'd been thinking that, although it'd be easy to blame Jehovah for all this, that that's not the case, of course — we got ourselves into this. And I was thinking that we'd have to use a lot of common sense to get ourselves out. So when I looked up and saw you being so full of common sense — it made me smile."

Some woman.

In the late morning sun, sitting in the hard dinghy with the mast across its sides, for over an hour I sawed away at the fiberglass pole with my dive knife. I thought about how

I would go about taking a sun shot if I could have. I would've waited 'til we got to the top of a wave, sighted on the next swell, then just kept it sighted as we went down the swell, adjusting to keep the sun in the other mirror and, after a few times, I'd get it so the sun would be in one glass the instant we started over. It'd take a few tries but I'd get it. Then I'd adjust for height of eye, half the height from crest to trough.

Every once in a while I'd look at my watch — we all had our watches — and think over and over how I'd shoot the sun in twenty foot swells. Noon came and went.

Finally sawing through, I now had two six foot lengths of fiberglass mast. I began to cut down the windsurfer sail to a size I could stretch between them.

"Bob, can you cut that sail so there's enough left over for a cover? Something to put over us at night?" Margaret quietly asked.

"Uhh... that'd be good," I told her, "but a little tough. I need a rectangle about three and a half by four and a half. Cutting it out of this triangle will leave uneven sections."

"Then I'll have to cut what's left and sew the pieces together, that's all. That's fine. We have the sail mending kit."

"This is four ounce dacron. It won't be easy sewing it."

"I'm not gonna spend another night with water splashing on me and wind blowing on me. I'll make a cover."

She said all this in a soft voice, not her usual, bubbly self. I couldn't be sure, but I thought she was feeling guilty. Not for the lack of supplies — well, maybe there was some of that — but if I had to guess, it would be that she had been on watch when we wrecked. I climbed into the Avon with her. "You know what I realized?" I asked. "When Chris and I were down on the reef, every part of it was under water. Three or four feet."

"Yes?" she replied, her head down.

"Well, it occurred to me that you couldn't have seen it while you were on watch. Certainly not at night, maybe not even in the day. Nobody could."

She looked up at me, her face a mask.

I said, "No way anyone on watch would have seen that reef."

"I could have seen breakers. Phosphorescence. Something."

"There was chop, wasn't there, in all that wind? White water?"

"Sure."

"Nobody would have seen that reef."

She looked down again, took a deep breath. "Give me the sail. If we're gonna square-rig it, it needs something to hold it on the masts." She started sewing a narrow sleeve on one of the short ends of the new little sail.

Chris and I readied the hard dinghy for the double masts. The sides of the Sandpiper had, next to the oarlocks, circular cup wells to hold drinks. These would hold the two mast-poles. We ran lines from the eyebolt in the bow to the two mast tops. Then we ran lines from the mast tops back to two more eyebolts in the stern. We could tighten these once the sail was rigged. It seemed like a lot of rigging for the tiny boat.

But the masts still had to be held apart to stretch the sail. Looking around for something to press into service, I hit upon the wind generator propeller. I hadn't taken any notice of this before because it had seemed useless. We'd kept it stored in the dinghy to get it out of the way. A wind propeller is used at sea to charge your batteries, since, in the middle of the ocean, you can't just pull into port to get a charge the way you can when you're sailing around

Catalina. The propeller is rigged facing the wind, connected to the generator. You run a line to your batteries and let the wind do the work.

I took this wood propeller and cut two half-circle grooves in its ends. This we'd use as a spreader above the sail to keep the masts standing apart. Chris brought out a red sweatshirt of his and we rigged it topmost. Red: international distress signal. Well, it was another little something, anyway.

Since Margaret was seeing slow going with the sail sleeves, I tried to figure out how our little fleet would respond to one craft having a sail and the other not. The soft dinghy, lashed alongside, would drag the Sandpiper sideways. Not workable.

"Chris," I said. "Let's try lashing the dinghies stern to stern. Then the sail will pull both in a line."

As we started to make it so, Margaret added, "And why don't you put out the windsurfer behind both, to stabilize?"

That seemed like a good idea. We could tow it upside down, too, so the non-skid surface would give a little more drag to keep us in line.

"And," Chris said, "we could put the sail sock out behind that and we'd really have a sea anchor."

Another good idea. So by the time Margaret had the sail ready, we had the dinghies lashed stern to stern with the Sandpiper's bow facing ahead, and a life preserver cushion stuffed and lashed between them to prevent chafing. The soft Avon faced the following seas, the surfer trailed on its twenty foot gold braid line, and a few feet behind this came the white fifteen foot sock, open to the water before it, looking like a benign python bringing up the rear.

We rigged the sail, made the bow and stern lines taut, inserted the propeller strut, and felt the wind take us forward smoothly. I climbed into the rear dinghy, facing Margaret in what was now the stern, and beyond her the following seas. Christian climbed in beside me as I took up the oar, put it through the oarlock and into the water, and began steering us west-northwest.

"Well," Margaret said.

"Very well," I said.

"Real good," said Chris.

SEVEN

*El Niño.... The massive warming kills many fish and
sea birds by preventing nutrient-rich cold waters
from rising to the surface.*

— *The World Book Encyclopedia*, 1993 Edition

*Without food, the energy needed to maintain essential
body processes, such as metabolism, is supplied by
substances stored in the body. About six hours after the
last meal, the body starts to use glycogen (a
carbohydrate stored in the liver and muscles). This
continues for about twenty-four hours, after which,
while the body adapts to obtaining energy from stored
fat, protein from the breakdown of muscles is also used
as an energy source. After a few days, most energy is
obtained from fat, although some continues to come
from muscle breakdown.*

— *American Medical Association Encyclopedia of Medicine*

Day two
November 11, 1982

At dawn, I nudged Chris awake and handed him the rudder. I undid a couple of the strings Margaret had used to attach the new cover, freeing my legs, and turned to crawl forward to the hard dinghy. I was almost getting used to the roller-coaster. The crossing from one craft to the other was still a wobbly affair, though. You had to crawl over the sterns on your belly. Make a mistake, lose your balance, and you'd be in the sea.

On my hands and knees, eyes just above the rigged sail, I looked forward and to both sides each time the dinghies crested, hoping to see some kind of land, though the chart didn't show anything in the area. One could hope. And maybe there'd be some kind of ship.

Then I sat on the seat of the Sandpiper, took the empty fruit cocktail can from the duffel bag, and started bailing. There were about two inches of water in the bottom.

Under the makeshift cover at the back of the Avon, Margaret stirred. She slid out from under it and smiled at me.

"That cover helped, huh?" she said.

"Yeah," I agreed. "Made a big difference." She'd attached it to the gunwales from the back of the soft dinghy almost to the front of it, tied it with sail thread through loopholes she'd punctured, and we'd all benefited from it. We'd all three spent the night in the far more comfortable Avon.

"Some water still got in," she said, undoing most of the ties and rolling the cover back, then lashing it, "but not that much." She sat back against it. "How'd you guys do?"

Chris said, "Not too bad. I'd sleep a couple of hours, then Dad'd wake me up and I'd hold the oar a couple of hours. There'd still be some splashing, but the wind wasn't as cold with the cover."

She said to him, "Do you want to try curling up back here tomorrow night? I'll sit next to your father."

"Oh, I don't know. Not unless you want to change. The steering is no strain, and you're the smallest." With a twinkle in his eye, he added "I'm the cutest, of course."

"You are not," she laughed. "Your father is."

"No, I'm the boldest," I said.

"Are we gonna eat, Bob the Bold?" Margaret asked with a smile.

"Yeah, I'll get it. You know, Honey, thanks for doing all that work with the cover. You had a bear of a time with it. Pushing a sail needle through dacron isn't easy."

"Yes, I know. My fingers are sore this morning." Without a thimble, Margaret had to balance the eye-end of the large, curved sail-mending needle against the hard dinghy, the sextant case, whatever, to push it through each time. The adhesive tape from the first-aid kit was all that made the vast patching possible. "Great stuff, adhesive tape!" she'd said. When finished, she slid the needle through the fabric above her breast pocket, and sighed with relief. "I bet this'll come in handy for a whole bunch of things."

Margaret slept fitfully through the night, curled up at the bow of the Avon, completely covered with the tied-down sail. Chris and I had sat side by side, facing her and the ocean beyond her, with our legs stretched over and around her in the cramped space. The interior of the soft dinghy was six feet, ten inches (I'm almost six feet tall) by two feet, four inches — less than half my outspread arms. The inflated sides cut down on the room a lot.

I stowed the can in the soaked duffel — I hadn't made much of a dent in the water level but I could come back to it — and got out a new can of food. We'd stowed all our supplies in the Sandpiper. There was certainly no room for anything but us in the soft dinghy. The supplies were all good and wet.

I put the can and can opener down the half open top of my wet suit and crawled back to the others.

"What do you think it'll be, Dad?"

"Do you want me to use my x-ray vision or the can opener?"

"I think the can opener, superguy. No offense but I think it'll work better."

As the lid came up, I said, "It's corn. You know, all these cans will have fruit packed in syrup or vegetables packed in water. Which we can drink. Maybe it wasn't such a bad thing, Margaret, all these cans."

"Good. Yeah. I'm glad," she said. I smiled at her and she smiled back.

"I'm starving, you two," said Chris.

I said a prayer for us. The corn was good.

We saved a few kernels to use as bait for the simple fishing tackle. It struck us funny, though, that we didn't see any fish about. No fish, no whales, no sharks, even when we'd been on the *Vamonos*. I'd always read that shipwreck victims survived, some even a hundred days, catching fish, turtles, hitting them with oars, spearing them. But we didn't see any.

"Well, we missed our check-in last night on the Maritime Net," I said.

"And come ten o'clock this morning, we'll miss check-in for the second time on the cockroach net," said Margaret. "Tom and Mary and the others will worry. They'll do something."

Chris said, "They know our last position. They'll figure the drift from there. They'll come and find us. We'll be back in Tahiti in a couple of days."

"Well, son, I doubt if we'll go to Tahiti. Our boat is wrecked — I think we'd go back home."

"What?! I wanna go to Tahiti! I wanna see the Castell family."

I finally tumbled on to it, why he'd been so unusually cheery even for him. "You didn't mind the trip being stopped, did you?" I said.

A little shame-faced, he said, "No."

"Why?" Margaret asked, shocked.

"Because. You and Dad promised! You said we would spend the hurricane season in Tahiti. Everything was great. I was in that school. I had friends I could surf with and kid around with, cool people — people my own age. I had Titaua..."

We were both surprised now. "Titaua Castell??" She was a beautiful, young, French-Tahitian girl. "What about her?"

"I stayed over their house one night. We stayed up talking all night. We were all in that little bedroom, her sister and her and me. And from that first night, we talked about everything, we got along so well, and her family are Witnesses... and she's so beautiful."

"What are you saying?" asked Margaret slowly.

"I'm in love with her. I thought maybe I'd stay. Maybe marry her."

"Chris, I think your dad will agree that you're much too young to be thinking about that."

"Yeah! Dad'd agree, all right! 'Cause Dad doesn't give me any freedom — just like you don't give me any respect."

"Chris," I said, "you don't know the meaning of love yet."

"Yeah, I don't know anything. I'm just a kid. Well, I'll tell you something: when we wrecked and I went down to get my stuff, you know what I got? The first thing was my survival knife but the second thing was her picture. She gave me her picture and a silver chain. I gave her a gold chain. Before I took any clothes, even, I took her picture! You went off to Bora Bora and I was happy in Tahiti! And then you came back and I went down to meet you and then, calm as could be, you said, `And you'll be coming with us to New Zealand.' Just like that."

"Chris," I said. "We wanted to all be together."

"Well, we're together now."

"Yes..." I said slowly. "But I can't see any way we could go back to Tahiti."

He looked at me, glared at me, but there were tears welling in his eyes. I couldn't think of anything else to say. He abruptly twisted and climbed forward into the Sandpiper.

We all were quiet for quite a while.

I'm hard headed and pragmatic, and I've been successful at it, all my life. I'd run my own business well enough to take two years off, at the age of fifty, to sail the sea. Now I was going to see if I was tough enough to do something really difficult, like handle a heart-broken seventeen year old.

I climbed forward to the Sandpiper. Christian didn't look up, but he knew very well that I was there; crawling into the little boat brought a lot of jerky motion with it.

"Chris, I didn't know that staying in Tahiti meant so much to you. I didn't know about Titaua." He looked up with a sad face.

"But when we get out of this mess, you can write her,

can't you?"

"I guess I could," he grumbled quietly.

"It'd be a good thing to do, anyway. You'll find out more about each other."

"We already know a lot."

"Sure," I said.

"Seeing her is what I want. Hearing her voice."

"Yeah, well still, I can't see how we could go back there now. Can you?"

He thought about that. Then he said, "No, I guess not."

"I have to be honest with you, son. Even if I had known about Titaua, I think I would have said she wasn't enough reason for us all to change our plans to staying in Tahiti."

"You see, that's just what —"

"Wait a second, let me finish. You have to realize that traveling together makes us, well — what one does affects the others. And if something new pops up for one of us — we're not a bunch of strangers on a cruise; we're a family. What I was going to say was that I would've thought that you were too young to rush into a close relationship, certainly too young to get married. But that if you wrote to each other and the relationship developed, that would be different. That and if it could stand the test of distance. And time."

"So, I'd've ended up writing her from somewhere else, even if this hadn't happened."

"It looks that way, yes." He looked at me with those sad eyes, but some of the tension had gone out of his face. "You know I love you, son. I want the best for you."

He looked out across the waves. "I love you, too, Dad. I guess it's all right."

"We really need to pull together, now. I mean, look

where we are. I'm gonna need you, need your help."

"Yeah. Sure." My son smiled a little. "I'm okay."

"Good. In fact, I think I'm gonna need your help immediately. This wet suit is starting to really chafe me. Do you think you have anything I could wear?"

"I don't know. A big hulk like you would probably split the seams."

———————————

Margaret said, "Look guys, I have this Mary Kay lipstick that was in my pocket. Seems to me it'll make a good sunblock for our noses and lips. What do you say?"

What I said was, "I'll try it." I took the palette of lipsticks and, using a pretty ordinary shade of pink, put some on my lips and nose.

"Put some on your cheekbones, too," said Margaret. "Chris? Try some?"

"Okay." Chris put some on, a lighter pink, and handed the palette back to Margaret. As she was putting some on her nose, Chris looked at me and began to laugh. I looked at him and knew what it was. He said, "The circus is in town."

I started laughing, too. "Clowns at sea!"

We all laughed. It was good for us. I probably looked more clownish than anyone. Chris's T-shirt was not a problem. He liked them oversized, and I'm slim. But his trousers were short for me and too tight. Margaret had taken the beige corduroys and split the seams all the way to the waist. Then she'd sewn in side panels of ace bandage from the first aid kit. They were silly but they were much more comfortable. The wet suit, laid out, became a flooring to put our life preservers on. The bottoms of the dinghies were always getting splashed, and it was good to not be sitting in water all the time.

―――――――――

Toward midafternoon, I had already tightened up the lines lashing the dinghies twice. Because of the constant, relentless motion of the sea, the cushion acting as a fender between the two craft would work up or down or sideways. The ocean never stops, calm or stormy. It was worst in the afternoon. The sea was always higher, brisker, then. We'd wrap and re-wrap the lashing lines with some of Chris's shirts — he'd had a whole bunch of them in his bag — to prevent chafing between them and the dinghies. We did some repair on the sail cover where sections had come apart during the night. We bailed the dinghies.

I got the first aid supplies and pulled out the sterile pads in their paper packages — why do they pack them in something that soaks right through? — and the bandages. They all were soaked, so I lay them out along the tops of the Sandpiper's gunwales. Our jackets were already tied, drying minimally, to the sail masts. From the duffel I took the big, cylindrical flashlight and opened it. Soaked. I removed the batteries and the bulb assembly and spread them all out on the seat. I unholstered my knife, but it seemed dry enough, so I put it back in the duffel. I took off my tennis shoes and set them down.

"Margaret, do you want to dry your..."

The ocean picked us up and threw us sideways. The dinghies hit the water and wheeled over. I was underwater with objects cutting past me, the bandages, slower than the rest, wriggling past like eels. I kicked for the surface and broke as we approached the trough of the wave. The soft dinghy was nearest me now and I grabbed for its side-strung lifeline. "Margaret! Chris!!"

"Dad! Over here!"

"Me, too!" They were on the opposite side of the Avon, coughing and hanging on. We soared on up to the crest.

Three sterile pads were right in front of me, stuck to the dinghy as we neared the crest of the next wave. A lifejacket floated to my right. I reached for it, yelling, "Grab anything you see!" After a moment, Chris called back, "Nothing over here but two of the lifejackets."

Oh no. "All right. Let's right the dinghies. This one first. You two pull down and I'll flip it over you — on three: one, two, three!" Scissoring my legs for stability, I heaved the Avon up and over them. That revealed my wet suit top and bottom, floating. I threw them up and in and the lifejackets and sterile pads followed. The Sandpiper had turned with the Avon.

I thought, *Sharks*. I put it out of my mind.

"Let's get in at the same time, for balance." We did that, caught our breath, then took stock.

We'd lost an oar, leaving us two; one had been lashed, the other had stayed in the oarlock. Most of the sterile pads and bandages, also some antibiotics, were gone; my tennis shoes, gone; the flashlight too.

The duffel had been tied, so it was there. Likewise the

down jackets, tied onto the masts. The pillowcase with the food and the five-gallon can had been tied. Thank God.

"Margaret!" I said. "You still have your glasses on."

"Yes. Wire bows. You know, the arms. They stayed wrapped around my ears."

"Amazing."

"Nice to find a good product," she grinned. Yeah, well, she was a good product herself. I would have thought that if I had to choose whom to be shipwrecked with, I'd have picked a couple of strong, sea-knowledgeable men. But what was called for, I began to see, was toughness. And a positive spirit. And my wife had those things.

So did my son. "Chris, we'd better re-rig the sail. The masts have come out of the sockets.

"Hey, Margaret? I love you."

EIGHT

A life raft is a life raft and a dinghy isn't. A life raft has a canopy, for one thing, which can be sealed with a zipper or by other means. That would have made a nice difference. Some have double tubes, too, making up the sides, or gunwales. That'll give you around nineteen inches of "freeboard" above the water line, reducing the amount of water that splashes in. Perhaps most important, I was beginning to realize, is the fact that a life raft has ballast in the bottom to prevent capsizing. And it's chock-full of survival supplies and flares and seasickness pills and things. It's a life raft! It comes in a canister. You open it, take out the raft, throw it in the water, pull a lanyard and it blows itself up. Had I really done the right thing — you never think you'll use the survival stuff — I'd've spent three or four thousand dollars on a life raft.

We weren't alone in this, though: Most yachties have dinghies, not life rafts. Most don't have money to burn; maybe they've sold their houses or have saved up for a lifetime. Sure, racing boats are owned by people with big money, but cruising boats are different.

And there was another thing about life rafts: They have no bows. Without a bow, you can't direct the thing with a tiller or a sail or anything; you'd just go around in circles. You float like a cork out there. That stuck in my craw.

The oar-rudder and the sail were the only really positive things we were doing to affect our future.

Chris started in with a Steve Martin routine to cheer us up. We'd heard this one before, several times before. It was still funny. The kid had such a sunny disposition; he'd get down, sure, but he'd bounce back again. A kid of good cheer. I detected something else, now, which was different from his usual approach to these imitations: On land and on the sloop, he had been doing it for the joy of being the entertainer, the performer. People watched, the guy who could crack them up. Now, I thought he was doing it to cheer us up, to contribute to the quality of our situation, to make things better. Interesting.

Around four o'clock we started our evening meal, if you could call it that. The peanut packs had around twenty nuts in each.

"Tell you what guys," Margaret said. "How about if I don't have any peanuts and you let me have a little more water?"

"Really?" I said. "They're delicious."

"What I want most is water. Six or seven peanuts don't make much difference, but I'm almost always thirsty."

"What about it, Chris?" I asked him.

"Fine with me." So that's how it would be.

Another thing our situation deprived us of was the sexual part of marriage, a regular, important part of my relationship with my wife. But curiously, as soon as we were thrown into this situation, my sex drive disappeared completely. It was as if the drive to survive, to get to land, overwhelmed other desires. Whatever the reason, my sex drive was nil.

On the other hand, our time spent praying and singing increased. Although we'd had our Bible discussions and daily prayers while on the *Vamonos*, the day before and again this day, we seemed to do these things more. Chris or Margaret had always occasionally said to me, "Say a prayer for all of us," and I would, praying aloud for the family. They'd do this much more frequently, now. And I know my silent prayers increased a lot. I think theirs did too, and I suspected this would all continue.

November 11, 1982
10:00 P.M.
Colin Busch home
Kawa Kawa, Bay of Islands
New Zealand

Colin Busch, a large man with a kind face that housed sharp, keen eyes, sat in front of his radio equipment. His wife, Janice, had made him his nightly cocoa, and he was sipping it contentedly as he listened to Mac in Hawaii running the standard communications on the Pacific Maritime Network. After giving the Hawaii weather and announcing that Bruce in Sydney and Colin in New Zealand were participating from their land bases, he asked for priority traffic, then began the check-in. The fourth boat he called, the *Vamonos*, failed to respond.

Mac, after a pause, said, "Has anyone heard from Kilo Alpha *** Quebec India India? Margaret and Bob? This is Bravo *** Delta Zebra standing by..."

There was a silence, which Colin finally broke with his call sign and: "Mac, what's this about Margaret and Bob?" Amid the standard signing in and signing off, a conversation which Colin found surprising emerged.

"Well, I can't raise them, Colin." There was a pause. "You weren't on the net the last two nights. They didn't check in last night, either."

"All right, but I've heard you handle situations like this before. It's usually, well, they must have a problem with their gear, we'll just give'em a stand-by.'"

"Right, and it's usually nothing to worry about — but if you look at the chart, they were very close to a couple of reefs, Beveridge and Haran."

"Yeah? I'll have to chart their last position, I haven't got out the chart and plotted it. But John, who I was staying with, has a little rig there so I just turned it on and I listened to their check-in. I heard the position report, so I have it written down. I'll plot it. But this happens, people go off the radio."

"Yeah, they do. Could be just the equipment."

Tom from the *Tashtego* called in. "I was waiting for you to get to my check-in, Mac, but I wanted to say to Colin that we have a little daytime net with the *Vamonos*, and Colin, I told Mac that we didn't hear from them yesterday morning. And I wanted to tell you both that we couldn't raise them this morning, either."

Bruce at the Sydney land base called in. "I don't know about this: They *were* in an area where there's a reef, two reefs. I think it might be wise to call up the commercial airline people, you know, suggesting that there could be a yacht with a problem out in the Rarotonga area. We could ask that they just make sure a good monitoring watch be kept for an epirb signal, in case an emergency beacon is being used out there."

"Colin here. Assuming they did put out an epirb signal, say day before yesterday night, you might find out if any commercial flights passed that way then."

"Right. They'd only turn one on if they spotted a plane. Otherwise the batteries'd wear down all too quick."

"Well, yeah, Bruce. But you know, they could be on the *Vamonos* even as we speak, sitting at their radio unable to send. You know, in an agony of frustration at hearing all this. Maybe they're cutting along toward the Kermadecs right now."

"Mac, here. Maybe you're right, Colin. I surely hope so."

"Right," Colin said. "But still, I'll plot the course for myself."

Causes of Dehydration. Even in a temperate climate, a minimum of three pints of water continues to be lost every 24 hours through the skin via perspiration, from the lungs into the air, and in the urine to rid the body of waste products....

In the initial stages of fasting, weight loss is rapid. Later, it slows, not only because metabolism slows down, but also because the body starts to conserve its salt supply, which causes water retention. Water that would normally be excreted in the urine is absorbed by the tissues.

— American Medical Association Encyclopedia of Medicine

*Day three
November 12, 1982*

"What about drinking urine, Dad?"

"They talked about that in survival class. They said don't do it. You took that class."

Margaret said, "But that never made sense to me. Supposedly, boat people do it all the time."

"I don't know," I said. "Anyway, I didn't urinate all day yesterday, I'm pretty sure. Yeah, I didn't." The first day we'd all discreetly chosen a moment, sat on the edge of one of the boats, pulled down our trousers, and defecated into the ocean. Then I, and I guessed the same for the others, had cleaned myself with handfuls of sea water, rinsing my hand afterwards. Urinating had been a lot easier, at least for Chris and me.

"What about you two?" I asked.

"I didn't," said Margaret.

"I didn't, and not number two, either," said Chris.

"None of us did," said Margaret.

I said, "I guess our bodies used all the moisture and all the nutrition. There wasn't any waste left over."

We'd just finished our morning meal. Green beans, I think it was, probably sliced French style, trés elegant. Less than six ounces each, including the water it came in. Then less than six ounces of water from the jug. Pretty accurately that much — It was amazing that there was no wrangling over rations. A one-for-all and all-for-one attitude had emerged. Maybe that would change, but for now we were doing well.

"Hey, look at that," Chris shouted. He was pointing to starboard but I didn't see anything.

Margaret twisted to look behind us and said, "Are those ours?"

"What?!" I still didn't see anything.

Chris said, "About thirty feet out. See? Two, no three red cans. Right, Margaret?"

"They look like our fuel cans," she said.

I finally saw. Three red five-gallon fuel cans were gaining on us, bobbing on the swells. We'd had three cans of fuel like those secured to the deck of the *Vamonos*. Spare fuel.

"Yeah, they do," I said. "I bet they are. I bet they're from the boat."

"They're going faster than us," said Chris.

"I wonder how they got loose," said my wife, always interested in details.

"Maybe being not quite full, the air in them made them fight their way to the surface," I guessed.

"Maybe the wreck shifted and cracked the deck more," offered Chris.

"Whatever it was, this is kind of eerie," I said.

We watched as the cans overtook and passed us, survivors of the same shipwreck, unthinking, headed nowhere.

Soon we got busy bailing anew and re-tying the lines between the boats, tying up our jackets to dry, all the things that we wanted to have done before the sea picked up in the afternoon. We were a lot more cautious now, tying everything down after we used it, checking a knot here and there to make sure it was fast.

"Nothing ever really dries," said Margaret, her voice full of frustration. "It's the salt water."

"Yeah," I answered. "Remember on the boat we'd rinse down the lines and such with fresh when they had salt water on them? Otherwise they rot."

"I think the salt in the fabric just sucks the moisture out of the air, or something. My jeans are always damp and it irritates me. My shirt is starting to feel stiff."

"Take it off, the way Chris and I do. You could leave your bra on."

"It'd make me colder."

"How would it do that?"

"I hate the wind on my shoulders, you know that. Even at the beach I keep something on them."

"Yeah, you do."

"That sun during the day makes you feel so good, though, Margaret," Chris commented. "After shivering all night it's soo-ooo good." We all had pretty good tans and the partially overcast skies prevented too much exposure.

The long swells rose only about four or five feet, as they had the two previous mornings, giving us a smooth ride. The nights had been pretty much like that, too. It was the wind in the afternoon that kicked the sea up. Not only would the swells get higher and higher, but the smooth crests would become like pyramids. When those crests hit us, it was with a jerk, then we'd lurch back toward the trough behind us, shooting down at about four knots. Then it was more difficult steering, keeping the dinghies straight to the waves so they wouldn't capsize us. That's why we wanted to get things done early.

I stopped what I was doing and stared, unseeing, at the bottom of the Avon. "I'm so sorry I got you two into this..."

"Bob, we're in this together. It's all right"

"No. No, it's not. We're stranded at sea. I should have been a better navigator. And I should've hove to for the night, not tried to sail through the dark!"

"We sail at night all the time, Bob."

"Not in dangerous waters. I knew those reefs were out there." A weakness seeped into my frame. "I just thought it was a million to one we'd hit them. In all that ocean, hitting them was like finding a needle in a... in two haystacks. But I should have been cautious."

"Aw, c'mon, Dad..."

"And this was my dream, sailing the Pacific. Not yours, Margaret, and certainly not yours, Chris."

"It's all right, Dad. We had fun. We had lots of fun — remember in Puerto Vallarta?"

I didn't answer him. I didn't even look at him.

"Look, Dad, you were the captain of the *Vamonos* and, yeah, you got us into this. But you're still captain and you'll get us out. It's cool, really. It's cool."

He made me feel a little better. I didn't deserve it, but it sure helped.

Our bottoms were beginning to hurt. We sat in salt water. We'd try kneeling every now and then, but mostly we sat. Sat in water.

Although we each, from time to time, would crawl slowly, carefully forward to the hard dinghy to be alone, it was getting very uncomfortable to sit there. So most often we'd sit in the little Avon, the three of us, trying to find places to put our limbs. In our usual configuration, Margaret sat in the "stern", dealing with my feet and Chris's. His feet would be pushed next to her thigh or on it. Mine, on her other side, would stretch past her, one on top of the other, or one up on the gunwale. In the daytime, Chris and I could draw up our knees for a change of position, but at night, the tied-down cover prevented that. Chris and I leaned against the Avon's moveable thwart in the true stern, lashed to the Sandpiper. We'd partially deflated the thwart — we needed the room. Sometimes we rolled over on our sides, rearranging our legs and feet. But as I said, mostly we sat.

"It's not just muscle soreness on your bottom, you know what I mean?" Margaret said. "It's a stinging."

"Must be the salt water, constantly on the skin," I said.

"Well, my upper body's usually wet, too, and I don't feel the stinging there."

"My feet are kinda irritated," added Chris. "Besides my butt."

My elbows were irritated, for some reason. Extremities. Well, your bottom isn't really an extremity.

"For me," said Margaret, "I feel some irritation on my feet."

In the afternoon we ate our peanuts and drank our water while the wind kicked the waves up to twenty feet. After that, we just rode it in silence. My silence had a lot of brooding at its heart.

Suddenly, Chris threw his hands up in the air and shouted, "Stop the water! I'll talk!" Now, *that* was funny.

Toward evening, I was at the tiller while the others were untying the shirts and jackets from the Sandpiper's masts. We'd need them for the night. Margaret and Chris had bailed out the dinghies, after the heavy seas, as best they could. It was quiet — the even swelling and falling of the ocean doesn't make much noise. Ready to unroll the handmade cover from where it was secured at the back of the Avon, Margaret crawled past me toward the "stern." Chris followed and was just coming abreast of me, with one leg still in the hard dinghy, when I heard the sound of a wave breaking — just like you hear at the sea shore. Looking behind at the following sea, I suddenly saw white water at the crest of a wave.

"Rogue wave! Port side!" It rammed the Avon amidships, throwing us back and to the side, with the Sandpiper following immediately. We were over, under the water, tumbling and fighting for control. I centered on the light of day next to the dark mass of a dinghy, twisted to face it, and kicked for the surface.

"Bob?" I heard.

"Dad?!"

I answered them. All accounted for. We gasped for a moment. We got the dinghies righted. We got inside.

We hadn't lost anything this time. The wind bit into us, chilling our clothes. We got the cover unrolled and huddled together under it.

I'd been watching the stars, Betelgeuse and the rest of Orion, when the clouds closed again. Chris had nudged me awake about a half hour before and given over the tiller. Next to me, he snored lightly. I couldn't hear Margaret but, under the cover that came to my waist, I could feel her with my legs. I shifted slightly to a more comfortable position. My bottom was sore. My legs were beginning to sting, now, too.

I heard a wave breaking. No, not again — it's relentless! A luminescence sparkled to port.

"Rogue!!" It hit us. Over again, into the water. Where's the surface? Dark, dark everywhere. Which way? I'd got a good lungful of air as I went over. I slackened my body and let the air take me up. Breaking the surface, I called, "Chris! Margaret! Sound off!"

A moment later I heard a splash, then, "Dad! Margaret!"

"I'm here. Margaret? Margaret!"

Chris yelled, *"Margaret!!"*

I swiveled my head frantically. Did she hit her head on something? It was dark. Not black. I could see a little. "Look for her on that side," I yelled. I let go with one hand and turned outwards, hanging onto the lifeline, peering quickly from left to right and back again. Nothing. Nowhere. "Do you see her?"

"No! Nothing! Where is she?"

I was holding onto the Avon. Maybe the Sandpiper had hit her on the head. I swung along to the hard dinghy, took a breath and pushed myself down under it. Black down there. I stretched out my hand and felt around — I was about two feet below the surface — nothing. I curled and kicked downward toward the bow but hit nothing. I reversed and swam an arc going aft, the wide strokes making no contact. I came up, gasping, and yelled, "Do you see her?"

"No!"

"Let's look under the Avon," and without waiting, I pushed myself under and back. Something moved in the blackness. I stretched out my hand and felt a leg. Clutching it, I realized it was pushing back toward me. Suddenly, it lurched past me and Margaret was turning. I let go of the leg and watched her swim past me. I broke the surface just behind her.

"What... What happened?!" I managed.

"I was trapped under the cover," she said. "C'mon, let's get the dinghies righted. I'm scared of sharks."

We did what she asked, but then I urged, "Honey! Tell us what happened!"

She said, "I was completely disoriented. I'd been asleep, and I didn't know what had happened! I was still on my side with the cover around me, sort of. It was so black — but there was air! I just didn't understand what had happened. I'd been asleep, you know? Then I realized we were over, but I was still under the cover. And I thought, I have to get out but I can't rip the cover. It's barely holding together, right? — and I didn't want to rip it apart. We need the cover! So I slowly started wriggling back, bracing on the sides as much as I could."

"You could breathe?"

"Yeah, there was an air pocket. Then I thought you might try to turn the boat over if you knew where I was and I knew you couldn't do it without ripping the thing. I was almost out when I felt your hand. I got so frightened for a second! Then I knew it was one of you and I pushed out past so you wouldn't try to pull me."

"Honey. Honey, we were so worried."

"Thought we'd lost you, Margaret."

"Oh thanks, guys. I'm all right. Really. And so is the

cover, not too much worse for wear."

"You know," said Chris, "if it's you or the cover, we can put together another cover."

"Hey, I *made* that cover."

———————————

"This Niño was a maverick: It behaved differently from recent predecessors. That's one reason we didn't recognize it. Another reason was a trick of nature. When it was first stirring in spring of '82, the Mexican volcano El Chicon belched an immense volume of dust into the atmosphere. The alien material misled our satellite sensors...."

— Dr. Eugene Rasmusson
National Oceanic and Atmospheric Administration
National Geographic, February 1984

Day three, evening
November 12, 1982
Colin Busch home
Kawa Kawa, Bay of Islands
New Zealand

Colin was at his radio, listening to Dave on the *Karana*, amid the usual radio protocol, answering his query. "The reason we changed our heading today, Colin, was the same reason we corrected it yesterday. We took some sun shots and they showed us much farther north than we'd thought. We'd figured to just get on the usual southwest currents and ease on down there toward the Kermadecs, then Bay of Islands, but it wasn't happening. Our position now, as you probably heard me tell Mac, is twenty-four degrees south latitude, 167 degrees west longitude. So we're heading southwest all right, but on a reach instead of having the wind and current directly at our backs. The sea is always shifting around, the wind too, but has anybody else been seeing currents they think are peculiar?"

Colin said, "Nobody's remarked on anything, Dave. Things are always shifting, as you say, and I don't know that anything peculiar is going on. I'll keep an eye out, though. So, Dave, what with Margaret on *Vamonos* not coming up on the radio, I had an idea earlier. You're following them. From the position you just gave, I'd say you'll soon pass a little south of Beveridge and Haran Reefs, is that about right?"

"I'd say that's right, Colin."

"Tom on the *Tashtego* is your buddy ship, right? Well, if you guys have got a little bit of time, why don't you make a pass near Haran Reef and just make sure there's nobody sitting there waiting for you to come by?"

"Tom here, Colin. What you have to realize is, those reefs are so small, you can't really know where they are. You could sail around there for hours, days, and never find them."

"Yeah, Colin. We were talking about it earlier and Tom said even if the reefs were above the water line, you can only see about two and a half miles around you before you reach the horizon. That is, if you're at sea level and the thing you're looking at is at sea level, not a mountain or something. And these things may be submerged, besides."

"And Tom and I discovered another thing, Colin. My chart doesn't show the reefs at the same coordinates as Tom's does. Mine has a note that Beveridge was reported in 1921 but his, with the different positions, doesn't note the report date. There's obviously some confusion about where those things really are."

"I see what you mean, guys. And different coordinates, eh? That's amazing. Listen, you two talked to Margaret that same day we had their last transmission, right?"

"Dave here. Yeah, our first day out of Rarotonga."

"Right then; so they seemed fine to me when I listened in, in the evening. Seem that way to you earlier in the day, did it? No problems?"

"Uh, Dave here. Well, they did say they had taken a few sloppy seas over the side that morning and — you don't know the *Vamonos* do you? See, the radio isn't particularly well-placed. If some water got down the companionway, they could have taken water on the radio."

"Oh, I see. Right, right. That could be it, then. Well, okay. Their radio patch could still be open to receive, though. Hmm. So, anything else, then?"

"That's about it for me, Colin. Naturally we're keeping a weather eye out for them as we move along. Maybe they've even hove-to, hoping we'd catch up with them so they could let everyone know they're all right. It's a very outside chance in all this ocean that we'd run across them, but maybe. We'll be on the lookout. Anyway, this is Tango Tango *** Lima Bravo Echo, clear with Pacific Maritime Net."

Tom signed back in asking for and getting the land base in Sydney, Australia. "Bruce," he said, "last night you mentioned that you might call the commercial airlines people and have them keep an ear out for an epirb signal. Did anything come of that?"

Bruce came back, "No, Tom. I called them just an hour ago and there still hadn't been anything. The official I talked to said something awfully bright. He said, 'It's a big ocean.' But they'll keep their pilots' attention on it. He assured me of that and I believe him. He didn't seem the careless type."

Tom signed off and Colin stated his call sign.

"Right, then. Have a good sail. Clear with Tango Tango *** Lima Bravo Echo and Hotel Charlie *** Foxtrot Bravo Charlie. So, Margaret, Kilo Alpha *** Quebec India India, you may be listening and here's the forecast for the position I estimate for you. Skies mostly clear, winds steady at eighteen knots out of the east..."

NINE

DDT, to which we are all exposed these days through insecticide-contaminated foods, is a cumulative poison which is stored in the fat tissues of the body. During fasting, when the body starts to feed itself on its own tissues, fat is broken down and digested, releasing dangerous amounts of DDT into the blood stream....

Daily enemas, the extensive program of revitalizing skin activity, lots of walking and deep breathing, and the medicinal, protective effect of raw fruits and vegetable juices, broths, and herb teas — all these help to make your fasting safer, in respect to the release of DDT into the bloodstream.

— Paavo Airola, Ph.D.
Are You Confused?

Day four
November 13, 1982

Our bottoms were really sore. None of us could sit in the hard dinghy any more, too uncomfortable. But all of us sitting in the Avon cut down considerably the space we had to live in.

"It's the salt water that's making the skin feel so bad, I guess," I said.

"And look at Chris's face. It must be affecting his acne, too. You had just a few little pimples when we were on the boat, didn't you?"

"Your face is breaking out a lot," I said

"Honest Dad, I'm not eating a lot of sugar and fried foods — I swear it!"

You had to laugh.

"Dave and Jan and Tom and Mary are, what, five days out of Rarotonga, now?" I asked Margaret.

"Four days, plus... that's right, five days."

"So after that first morning, they haven't heard from us for five days. One of them must be saying, `Hey, something's wrong.'"

"I keep looking at the sky for a plane — y'know, a rescue plane."

"Me too. Or a ship."

Chris looked up from the fishing lines. "Hey, Dad, this plastic lure's not getting anything. Wanna try one of the metal ones, the shiny ones?"

"Fine, Chris," I said. Why were there no fish?

"I'd really like a broiled lobster," Chris mused. "You know? A lobster and a filet mignon. With a pepper on it. And butter! Remember the steaks in Bora-Bora with butter on them? Oh yeah."

———————

Our days were taking on a routine of sorts. Up at dawn, with a prayer to Jehovah for getting us through the night. Then breakfast, sharing the one can of food, then the can of water. Bail the dinghies; pump up the inflatable Avon, to replace some air it lost; re-tie the lines holding the dinghies together while adjusting the cushion between; check the sail for tears; tighten the rigging. Make sure of all lashings on supplies. Discuss the Scripture in the *Yearbook,* listen to Margaret reading aloud the experiences of our brothers from one of the other sections. Sing some songs. Periodic solo trips to the hard dinghy for a little solitude — and to allow the other two more room in the Avon. Talk about good times, talk about food. Some Steve Martin from Chris. Songs. A surprising number of smiles.

———————

I was sitting, washing off my dive knife, which I'd used to trim some rough edges on the fiberglass masts. Holding the blade in both hands, I lowered it over the side. I rubbed the metal, underwater, between my palms, keeping a steady pressure on it. Suddenly it backed out of my grip and was gone. My jaw dropped.

The night of the wreck leaped to my mind. The coconuts in their bag, the new, strong net bag, spilling into the sea for no reason. Just like the dive knife.

The sea took them, I thought. First the coconuts, now my dive knife. It took them away from me.

———————

A couple of hours after sundown, we tied down the cover and Margaret curled up in the "stern" and went to sleep. She's a champion sleeper.

Even out here, she sleeps two or three hours at a time, wakes up, says "Who's there?" and whoever's awake at the rudder will answer her, she chats a little, then goes back to sleep. She told me that she never really had good sleep, though. You can never quite relax out here. You're always somewhat tense. I asked her if our moving our feet during the night bothered her. She said it woke her but that that was all right — "It's very important to feel your touch," she said.

I'll stay awake as long as I can. Then wake Chris to take the oar. What's that over to the right...? A fin! Is that a fin?? A shark?? Gone. Could it have been a shark? There had been no fish at all. Would there be sharks where there were no fish? Nothing there now. Relax.

But she's right: You never relax.

———————

Day five
November 14, 1982

Mid-morning and I was at the tiller. I was tired. I hadn't slept much the night before, hadn't felt that sleepy, so I'd kept the helm most of the night. One little catnap.

I stared at the following sea, monitoring for white water, for a rogue wave. The sea. It was being quiet, the way it did in the mornings. Not showing its power. Maybe it saved itself up for its vigorous times, for its violent times. Maybe it hummed to itself with pleasure as it rested, secure in its immense strength, pleased at its absolute advantage. Maybe.

It slid the oar from my hand. Shocked, I stared at my empty claw-grip, the muscles rigid, hard and hurting.

"Dad! The oar!"

I looked up stunned, to see Chris pointing at the water, the way sailors do when someone goes overboard.

Without moving his eyes, he said, "I should get it, right?!"

What? I thought.

"Dad! Get it, right?"

"Get it. Yes."

He dove in and swam strongly after the trailing oar which fell farther and farther behind us. When the gap was fifteen feet I thought he almost had it, but it seemed to elude him. Twenty feet. Twenty-five. He had it.

He turned in the water and started back. He wasn't making up the distance as easily as I thought he would. Suddenly, he stopped stroking and put his hands down into the water — why? He stroked twice, the oar grasped in one hand, and then reached down again, starting to bend over, sinking under the water. What was he doing?? He broke the surface again, drawing his knees up and sank again. Shark?! No, he'd be screaming. What was he doing?? He broke the surface again and started swimming toward us. I suddenly realized how far behind he'd got. It must be forty feet!

I leaped up and scuttled forward to the hard dinghy. I yanked the left mast out of its socket but the right one was too firmly lashed. I got to my knees and wrenched it with both hands; the sail came down. Picking up the second oar from the dinghy floor, I yelled to Margaret, "Paddle with your hands! We've got to get back to him!"

I dug the paddle into the water and paddled for dear life, my son's life.

We'd never tried going back against the following sea. It was so strong. I'd dig the paddle deep into it and push us, then as I brought the oar out it seemed to make up the difference. I put my head down and dug deeper. Then I started stroking frantically, small strokes, not letting the sea recover, harder, harder.

I looked up and Chris was closer. Less than twenty feet. He wasn't swimming well. Why? He's good! He had the oar in one hand, and that probably threw him off some, but still.

I dug in again. "Paddle, Margaret!"

"I am," she yelled. I tried to step it up, dig, dig...

It went on, went on, went on. My arms ached, pain on the left side of my back, arms ached, ached, I'll get weaker, no I won't, arms, arms, my son's life...

I heard something clunk into the soft dinghy. I whipped my head up, lungs heaving, and saw Chris's hand and the oar he'd swung into the boat. Margaret was pulling him by his shirt. I threw down my paddle and dashed back to them. I grabbed him under the arm and we hauled him aboard.

I realized I was crying. When did that start? I cradled

him and tried to get my face to his, but Margaret was already there, kissing his face, hugging him.

"Chris," I muttered. "Chris, thank God."

He was panting like a bear. We stayed there like that, me hugging Margaret hugging him.

"I couldn't... swim with my legs," Chris said between gulps of air. "My pants got so heavy... so I tried to get them off. They got stuck at my ankles. I couldn't get them off. I tried to swim anyway but now my feet were, like, tied together. Couldn't use them at all. Just my arms. Hadda hold the paddle, though. Hard. Very hard. Thought I'd drown. Really thought I'd drown."

———————————

That night we capsized.

TEN

Staphylococcal infections.... Bacteria are present harmlessly on the skin of most people. If the bacteria become trapped within the skin by a blocked sweat or sebaceous gland, they may cause superficial skin infections such as pustules, boils, abscesses, styes, or carbuncles. Infection of deeper tissues may result if the skin is broken.

Staphylococci, which grow in grape-like clusters, are a common cause of skin infections but can also cause serious skin disorders.

— *American Medical Association Encyclopedia of Medicine*

Day six
November 15, 1982
approximately thirty miles south of Niue Island

"Does your butt feel as bad as mine?," Chris asked me.

"If yours feels terrible, then yes," I said.

"I think I've got lumps," he said, leaning on his side and feeling his bottom.

Margaret, doing the same, said, "I've got lumps. Definitely lumps."

My inspection of my own bottom indicated the same sort of thing. I got on my knees, turned my back to them, and said, "Tell me what you see." I pulled down the pants top.

"They look like boils," remarked Margaret. "They're about the size of quarters and they're very red."

"They have little heads on them," Chris said.

"Great," I said.

"Take a look at mine," said Chris.

They looked terrible, angry, unhealthy. He had one or two all the way up near his waist, maybe eight on the buttocks, and three or four at the tops of his thighs.

"Better look at mine, too," said Margaret. I knew she was a little embarrassed, but you had to be real about this. She had trouble getting her pants down, though, because once she started, the small-waist of the woman's jeans rode tightly over her bottom. She screeched a little but got them down; she looked as bad as Chris had. Oddly, she had more on her right side than her left, and I told her so.

"Remember," she said, "I've been sleeping on my right side."

"This salt water is getting to us any way it can." I almost said, "any way it can think of." Ridiculous.

Still kneeling, Margaret had pulled the jeans past her panties and was looking at her thighs. "I have some small ones on my legs, too."

"Mine are on my hands," Chris said.

"My hands have been bothering me, too," I said, and looked them over. Sure enough, I had three or four small red bumps on my hands. One on my elbow, as well.

"My butt is what really hurts, though," said Chris.

"Let's do this," I said. "From now on, we'll always sit on the wet suit and the life jackets. You know, when we sit in the Avon we make a low point in the floor, and the water congregates there. We're sitting in little pools of salt water. So let's sit on things all the time."

They thought it was a good idea.

It also occurred to me that our bottoms, and in fact our hands and legs, were below our hearts. Less circulation. I didn't know if that was a factor.

"You know, Chris's acne is even worse."

He said, "I thought sun was good for acne, and a simple diet, too."

"I thought so, myself," I said.

Around noon, I noticed that the Avon was looking a little deflated, so I set Chris to pumping it up a bit with the foot-pump. It was sort of a bellows affair; you're supposed to just attach it and step down on it. Since we couldn't stand in the dinghies, he did it by hand. The Avon was losing some air through a patch. Some months before, Chris had dropped an anchor on the stern. Seems like patches on Avons never really take. It was a good thing that after he'd inflated it the last time, before abandoning the *Vamonos*, he'd had the presence of mind to throw the pump into the bottom of the boat.

We were so *hungry*! I hadn't known you could get so hungry. It was like I had a hard, wooden ball in my stomach all the time. When the morning food would go in, my stomach didn't welcome it. It was like the emptiness had become solid, and then food had no real place there. The canned food was comparatively easy to digest, fortunately, and soon the wooden ball would loosen up a bit. In fact, it was satisfying, and meals were the highlight of the day. But it was a short-lived satisfaction; later my stomach would revert.

And it hurt — no, more of an ache. It would start as a dull ache after the meal, quickly become a sharp pang, then lots of sharp pangs, then they would dull down, get denser and denser, and finally there would just be that wooden ball again, heavy, an otherness that I carried inside me.

We talked of food. I thought maybe it was a bad idea, but I was just as avid as the others about it. We talked of specific foods, we talked of combinations. We reminded each other of meals we'd had together and described ones we'd had apart. We made up dishes that sounded exquisite. I'd pay strict attention to their descriptions, really trying to taste the ingredients, relish the aftertaste. My best recipe, I think, was a dessert. It would have seven or eight very different flavors of ice cream: Swiss almond mocha, strawberry, vanilla, butter pecan, orange sherbet, things like that. I'd use a little scoop like the ones they use to make melon balls, and get a bunch of these different ice cream balls. But then I'd dip them in chocolate and freeze them all. Served in one of those wide, flat champagne glasses, you'd have maybe a dozen identical-looking chocolate balls, and each time you spooned one of them into your mouth, you'd have a surprise from a different flavor inside. We liked that recipe.

We'd talked of food from the very first afternoon in the dinghies. Our stomachs had been used to three good meals a day, and the first day was hard. The second day was worse. The third day was about the same, so I thought perhaps we'd get used to it.

The fourth day was a little better. But it never got better than that.

Late in the afternoon, we could see a squall coming. For the previous two days, off in the distance, we'd seen rain. The clouds would have dark undersides, then you'd see that space between them and the ocean get dark, and you'd know that was rain. "Why is it raining over there?" Chris said, more than once. "We need water here!" Now rain was coming.

"You and I will use the cover to catch water," I told Chris, starting to unroll it. "Margaret, what can you find to catch water off the sail?"

She already had it planned. She got the plastic box which housed the sextant, left the instrument itself on the floor of the soft dinghy and went forward to the Sandpiper. Chris and I undid the cover entirely and each held an end of it.

There were a few fat drops and then the squall hit with a passion. The sound of the rain thrumming on the dinghies was almost deafening. Rain poured onto us and onto the cover. Whipped by wind, it got there nevertheless; who cared if it came from above or from the side? We were soaked but that was okay with me. Let it rain! We had a little pool in the bottom of the cover already. We had the material maneuvered so that the lowest point was the largest unpatched piece. Lovely little pool. Grow. That's it. That's it. We can get enough for days this way.

Then the sea blew from behind us. A brief shower of flecked ocean. Into our pool. Poisoning it.

"Let it out," I yelled to Chris. Then: "Hold it sideways," and we let the pure water rinse the surface. "Okay, but now hold it higher!" We lifted our arms to eye-level and started again. The Avon's gunwale is only about fourteen inches — that was why it was always so easy for the sea to get into the boat. We'd been holding the cover down at our thighs, about the same height as the gunwale. No wonder we'd been splashed.

The rain poured down, a real South Pacific squall, heavy, large drops of pure water. My arms were beginning to hurt just a little, but it was worth it. Worse pain than this would have been worth it. Drinking water! Free. From the skies.

A shower of sea water hit my face and splashed on into the cover. It was beyond belief! I knew there was wind but...

We rinsed it off again. We held it up again. My arms ached a little, right away. No matter. Get the water. Drinking water. Water to live. How much should we get before we poured it in the jug? I lowered my end a bit to see how much there was. About two inches at the deepest part.

What was that? Two ounces? Maybe three. Maybe I should wait until it was twice as deep. Maybe, in fact, I should wait until it was full, in case the rain stopped suddenly. How long do these things...?

The sea belched in. Ruined. The freshwater was ruined. We rinsed off.

"Chris. Get the water can. Don't take the top off, just keep it closed. We'll get some rain and pour it in, get a little more, pour it in. Let's hold the cover higher."

Holding it up above our heads, the strain on the arms was worse. I wanted to stand, lower the cover to my chest, hold it there, but you couldn't stand. We'd tried it plenty of times in the last few days, and, even in the calmest weather, you had to crouch or kneel, you couldn't balance. No, standing was no good.

The wind buffeted us, blowing some of the rain in and some away. Just hold it. Get some in and pour it. We'll have to cradle the jug so that the sea has no chance to get to it. Oh, that would be a catastrophe. If the sea got into our supply. That —

A wave came plowing through.

And it went like that, time after time after time. As if the sea watched. As if it calculated when it had let too much of its cousin reach us. As if it reached forward in malice and fouled our drink of life.

A half hour later the squall blew past. Margaret, in the forward dinghy, higher up at the sail, channeling it with one hand into the sextant box in her other, had got eight ounces of water. We'd got none.

———————

10:30 p.m.
Colin Busch home
Kawa Kawa, Bay of Islands
New Zealand

"...Clear with X-ray Victor *** Baker Charlie Baker."

"So, Kilo Alpha *** Quebec India India — Margaret, hi there. This is the fourth evening I've broadcast to you, broadcast `blind' so to speak, and I certainly hope you're out there listening. We surely hope you are, Margaret."

"I've been plotting your course daily and, as near as I can reckon, you should be about 250 miles out from the Kermadecs, or at least from Raoul, northernmost in the group there. I know you'd be on a broad reach and don't know how much sail you'd be putting up, so maybe you're a bit farther on or not quite so far. But in any case, for that general area, I can give you some idea of the weather thereabouts, and I hope it'll be of some use to you. So for a position approximately 177 degrees west, twenty five degrees south, you should have partially clear skies, with the wind at..."

Mid-morning
Day seven
November 16, 1982
Past Niue Island

Margaret read, "'The fruitage of the spirit is love, joy, peace, long-suffering, kindness, goodness, faith, mildness, and self-control. Against such things there is no law.'" This was from Galatians. Our *Yearbook* was wet, but serviceable. She had to take a minute or so to carefully turn a page so as not to rip it, but it was holding together.

It was warm this morning, very little cloud cover, and the ocean was calm. Chris and I had our shirts off and pants down, lying on the gunwales of the Avon. The shirts and jackets, tied to the masts, flapped in the breeze, a truly ragtag sail. Hopefully they were drying a little. I'd suggested to Margaret that she try to get her jeans down, get some sun on her bottom to help with the boils, but she'd said the pain and strain weren't worth it.

The sun felt good, very good, on my bare skin. The rest I was getting was enormously welcome, too. I was getting weary. Every day the strength in my body, something that I was accustomed to having just be there, waned a bit.

Margaret said, "Should I read some more about the Witnesses in Italy?" Most people don't know that, during World War II, Jehovah's Witnesses were sent to prison by the Fascists and the death camps by the Nazis for refusing to go to war against their fellow human beings.

As she started, Margaret's soft voice belied the tone of terror that was inherent in the quotes from official Italian circulars quoted in the *Yearbook*. The one dated March 13,

1940, from the Ministry for Home Affairs, rang with both the treble tone of intolerance and the clang of suppressive might natural to a totalitarian government:

> *Jehovah's Witnesses' proclaim that both Il Duce and Fascism originate from the devil and that, after a period of short-lived victory, these phenomena must unfailingly meet their downfall.... No effort should be spared, therefore, to repress the slightest manifestation of this sect's activity.*

One sister, Maria Pizzato, was sentenced on five counts which went like this:

> *Five year's imprisonment for associating with a view to political conspiracy; one year's imprisonment for offending the dignity and prestige of the Duce of Fascism, Head of the Government; two year's imprisonment for offending the Supreme Pontiff; one year's imprisonment for offending the dignity of the Head of a Foreign State, Adolf Hitler; and two year's imprisonment for offending the prestige of the King and Emperor.*

Some parts of the story were particularly resonant, in light of our own circumstances. Brother Marcello Martinelli had written,

> *From November, 1939, to the end of February, I shivered with cold, because not only was the cell unheated but the window had no glass in it. I was not even given a change of clothing, and soon I was reduced to a miserable, repulsive creature afflicted with parasites.*

But some parts made what we were facing seem, well, not as bad as it might have been:

One day at the end of December, Narcisco Riet's house was surrounded, and an SS officer and his men burst in. Narcisco was arrested and kept at gunpoint while the soldiers searched the house. They soon found the 'criminal' evidence they were looking for — two Bibles and a few letters. Narcisco was sent on the long journey back to Germany [he had been born in the province of Udine] where he was imprisoned in Dachau concentration camp. There he was horribly tortured. For a long time he was kept chained up like a dog in a low, narrow cell. After much suffering inflicted in one camp after another, he was put to death before the Allies occupied Berlin. His remains were never found.

I believed those times of reading together and praying together were making us better at survival. I prayed silently during the day. Margaret and Chris did, too, I figured. Not glib prayers, either. There was nothing about our situation that lent to glibness. Being lost at sea had a wonderful way of focusing our attention — on survival, on exactly how we were doing in this respect or that, and on a prayer, asking for life to continue — continue for all of us. There was a growing feeling of togetherness, of being on each others' sides, come what may. You should have seen how meticulous we all were about not taking more than a third of the canned food, of not taking more than our share of the water. You should have seen how much we cared for each other.

———————————

Near midnight, I had the tiller. The sea was high, I didn't know why; it was usually at its least vigorous at night. I tried to gauge the height of the swells, but in the black of the overcast sky, it was hard. Maybe ten or twelve feet, meaning twenty or twenty-four from the trough to the crest. The others were sleeping, but I felt a strained sort of alertness. I realized my teeth were clenched, and I consciously loosened my jaw. I watched the following seas for signs of phosphorous, which would mean a breaking rogue wave. About an hour before, one had come up on my left and I had steered the dinghies quickly around and it'd hit us pretty square astern. We took some sea from the normal wave following it, but by the next swell, I had us back squared to the prevailing current.

You'd hear a breaking wave before you saw the phosphorous, sounding just like a wave breaking at the beach. Often you'd hear something, peer like crazy into the black, tense up, get ready to steer, but nothing would happen. Well, at least nothing would happen where we were. The rogue would break on through some other wave, somewhere behind or off the beam. Just a fright, nothing more.

Now I heard the crashing of the rogue and stared behind. We were headed down toward the trough. Nothing, nothing — then the sparkling head whacked us broadside from starboard and pitched us over.

Into the water. Chris's body bumped me hard and I grabbed onto him, wanting to keep him near. Would Margaret get out of the cover all right? Rip it if you have to, Margaret! I held Chris and tried to get my bearings, tried to know which way was up. He pushed away from me but I didn't think that was the way up, so I tightened my grip. Then my head bumped up into the side of the hard dinghy. I lurched backwards, gulping air into my lungs, pulling Chris to me. He suddenly was wriggling and kicking at my legs and I tried to pull him up. He wrestled free and a moment later I heard him gasping for breath on the other side of the Sandpiper.

"Chris, are you all right?!"

"*Yeah*, Dad... What were... you doing? Almost drowned me!"

"Bob? Chris?" Margaret called as she broke the surface.

"We're here! Grab the line! Chris, what do you mean? I was bringing you with me to the top."

"I could see the Sandpiper against the sky a little bit, and I was making for the edge. You kept pulling me in another direction."

"Oh! I'm so sorry. I didn't know."

He pulled himself to the top of the overturned dinghy and grinned at me. "You're killin' me with kindness, Dad."

Margaret called, "Can we get out of the *water*, please?!"

We righted the dinghies. The next day we discovered we'd lost the fishing lures. Not that they'd done us any good.

ELEVEN

Day eight
November 17, 1982
Three hundred nautical miles from Beveridge Reef,
180 nautical miles from Vava'u, Tonga

"Keep your eyes open, boys and girls," I said. "We should be seeing one of the Tonga islands about now."

"No way you're gonna see land," said Chris. I stared at him. Since dawn he'd moped through our maintenance, said hardly a word, sat now with hunched shoulders. We'd all only been up an hour. Chris had had the pre-dawn tiller duty. I asked him what he was talking about.

"No way you're gonna see anything in these seas. Don't think so. I don't know why you think we're near Tonga."

"Because I can see the direction we're going by the position of the sun, that's why."

"We're not near Tonga. We're not near anywhere."

Margaret said, "Chris, come on. What's the matter all of a sudden?"

He didn't answer. He started to climb forward into the Sandpiper.

"Chris," I said. "What are you doing? What's up?"

He stared at me. "Eight days? That's how long we've been out here? Eight days? It should be over. It should have been over days ago."

"But it's not. This is our situation — we have to make the best of it." That didn't seem like such a convincing argument, but he'd taken me so much by surprise.

"Chris," Margaret said, "this doesn't sound like you at all."

"Did you feel down the other day, Margaret?"

"Yes, and you tried to cheer me up. You did Steve Martin."

"Yeah, well, now I'm feeling bummed. Don't I have that right? Can't I feel what I feel?"

"Well, sure, sweetie, but..."

"So let's leave it at that."

"Son," I said, "if you were feeling like we were going to get rescued after just a few days, well, sometimes it doesn't work out so nicely. We've got to face what's in front of us."

"I don't want this to be what's in front of us."

"Come on, Chris. I need you," I said.

That again seemed to mean something to him. There was a pause.

"Yeah, well, I'm all right." He continued forward into the little Sandpiper.

"Thanks, Chris," Margaret said. "We depend on you. On your strength."

9:30 p.m.
Colin Busch home
Kawa Kawa, Bay of Islands
New Zealand

Janice walked into the room with a mug of cocoa and set it down on the desk. Uncharacteristically, she sat in one of the easy chairs nearby instead of going on with her nightly routine.

Colin didn't notice her looking at his face, frowning at the tension lines she saw around his month that weren't usually there. He didn't see her mild surprise when his voice revealed only the sound of his usual calm good nature.

"This is Zebra Lima *** Bravo Kilo Delta. Are you still out there, Hotel Charlie *** Foxtrot Bravo Charlie?"

Tom from the *Tashtego* signed back on. "Yeah, Colin, we're still listening."

"You said you're becalmed in the Kermadecs, presently. Now, we don't have any way of knowing if the wind was down a couple of days ago there, also. What I'm thinking of is that we've been figuring the *Vamonos* a couple of days ahead of you, which would make them just about making port. But now I guess we're gonna have to reckon that they may have got becalmed, too. But I hate to do that."

Colins jaw muscles clenched. In front of him he saw, not a radio console, but a vast ocean with a small boat in its grip, a small boat containing three tiny figures.

"This is Dave, Colin. I came up on Tom a couple of hours ago, using the motor toward the end. Now this is a cove here, but the waves are bouncing us around pretty good. You know, this close to land, the waves are still coming in, hitting the cove walls, and rushing out again. We're just a twenty-six footer, smaller than Tom's boat, and we're not sitting well at anchor. So, I'd already been thinking, maybe we'll motor on. That way, you could still use us as a yardstick for Bob and Margaret's arrival."

"Yeah, yeah, that's better, Dave. We can figure that the *Vamonos* might have motored on, too."

"One thing, though. A while back, they were having some trouble with their motor, only getting three cylinders."

Colin said, "Damn," under his breath, then got back on the radio. "Well, maybe we'll figure them for a healthy motor anyway, Dave. Could be they fixed it."

"All right, Dave. We'll use you as the yardstick. They should arrive before you. If they don't show up and you do, we can convince anyone that something's definitely wrong."

Dave and then Tom cleared with the Net. Janice Busch got up and touched her husband's arm. He looked up, surprised but instantly accepting her presence, and put his hand over hers. Janice remained standing there as her husband resumed on the radio.

"Zebra Lima *** Bravo Kilo Delta clear with Hotel Charlie *** Foxtrot Bravo Charlie and Tango Tango *** Lima Bravo Echo. Okay, then, Margaret, Kilo Alpha *** Quebec India India, the winds southwest of the Kermadecs are a steady twenty knots out of the east-southeast and the skies are clear..."

———————

Day nine
November 18, 1982
One hundred and fifty nautical miles
from Vava'u, Tonga

I visualized what it would be like to spot an island, land on it, drag the dinghies up on the beach and walk to a village. The natives would be amazed to see three bedraggled white people appearing in their midst. They'd give us papayas, some bananas maybe, coconuts to drink from and scoop the pudding from. All the fruit would be wonderful. They'd have some native remedy for salt-water boils, and they'd rub cool salve onto our fiery skin. They'd give us clean lava lavas to wear and we'd brush our teeth with toothpaste. We'd rest and then they'd take us in a big outrigger canoe to a main island where there'd be a radio...

"What's wrong with the radio network?!!" I burst out. "It's been nine days since they've heard from us! What are they doing? Where's the search plane? What are they, *stupid*?"

"Yeah," Chris said. "Where *are* they?!"

Margaret got angry, too. "Isn't this what the net is for? To know if we're lost and then get us saved? Isn't that the whole purpose?"

But as Chris and I went on in this same vein, Margaret calmed down. I think she figured if we were all going to get angry and negative, we'd be in bad shape — bad for the business of living.

"Maybe they are looking for us," she said. "Maybe they're out in boats instead of planes. In all this ocean, we're a very small pinpoint to find, when you think about it."

"Yeah, well maybe," I grumbled. Not with a lot of grace.

Day ten
November 19, 1982
One hundred and twenty nautical miles
from Vava'u, Tonga

"We should have reached Tonga by now, and since we haven't, maybe I was wrong that we're making two knots. Maybe it's more like one knot." We could measure nautical miles on our chart and a knot is the speed you go when you travel one nautical mile in an hour. I knew we could figure on a pretty straight line of travel because the wind and current travel straight, and the sun was pretty much in the same place, and we kept our rudder at a constant angle, close to the craft. "If it's one knot, then we're still a couple of hundred miles out."

"Oh, Bob, that's a good thought. That's probably it, we're just not going as fast as we thought." She said this with relief. She had been wearing a slightly haunted look since the day before.

"So we're gonna have to keep a sharp eye."

"We can't see much with these seas, Dad. And not very far, either."

"As a matter of fact, at sea level, you can see the horizon at about two and a half miles. That's not much, but an island rises above the horizon, so if it's got any hills or mountains, you see the tops of them from much farther away. Remember how we'd always see the palm trees first from the *Vamonos*, even with a flat island?"

"Yeah," he said. "Well, that's something at least."

_____

Chris said, "Forget the lobster and steak. What I'd really like is some ice cream. Or a sandwich. But definitely some ice cream."

That afternoon we finished the peanuts.

10:15 p.m.
Colin Busch home
Kawa Kawa, Bay of Islands
New Zealand

Colin listened as Mac went through the roster of maritime mobile units, getting positions, weather reports, exchanging information and pleasantries, when, during a routine check-in, the owner of the *Windtree* added, "There's something else which maybe you should know, Mac. Regarding the *Vamonos*." Colin's attention focused sharply on the transmission. "Maybe you should know that they've had one or two problems on the boat recently." There was a pause and then the voice continued, "Structural problems. Do you think that matters?" He gave his call sign and said he was standing by.

Mac came back and said, "Why don't you just tell us what you know, Harry?"

Harry was still hesitant. "Well, they had one or two little things, you know. They were taking on some water in Papeete. About a month ago. It's not a fiberglass hull, you know. It's fitted mahogany. I think they had some repair work done — but I'm not sure."

"Is that it, Harry?"

"Well, there was that thing with their motor — only running on two or three cylinders. I don't know if they had that fixed."

"Yeah, we know about that. Okay, does anyone else out there know anything else about the *Vamonos*? Anything about problems."

There was some dead air-space. After thirty seconds, Colin broke the silence. "Now, look folks, it's unfortunate that you have to talk about these things on the air. I know the yachting fraternity doesn't like to talk about anyone else's misfortunes, especially in public — but this might be vital data, or at least helpful in guessing what's going on out there. And if we have to make a case about this, which I'm beginning to think we may, we must know what's what. So. Does anyone else out there know anything about problems on the *Vamonos*?"

The two or three yachties who now called in did little more than confirm that there had been a problem with the hull taking on water, but the exact type of problem could not be nailed down. A minor problem that could unexpectedly turn into a huge problem might be cause for real alarm. But here, one just couldn't be sure.

Colin felt the frustration welling. What did they have to go on? No check-in but feasibly just a radio malfunction. Non-arrival but possibly just a becalmed vessel. The faster *Vamonos* not in yet when the slower *Karana,* having left two days previous, was drawing near. But still, no clear cause for alarm.

Mac said, "All right. I gather that's all the light anyone can shed. Well, they're running under some rough conditions out there. The current's not with them and the winds haven't been cooperative. And maybe the hull is giving them a problem and that's slowing them down too. Or they can't repair something and can't get any instructions over the radio. Hopefully they're somewhere between the Kermadecs and New Zealand. But under these rough conditions, it's also possible things got really bad and they had to abandon ship."

Colin came on the air. "I'd like to get a very detailed description of the *Vamonos*, from anyone and everyone out there who knows the boat, for possible use in an aerial search."

The airwaves were jammed for the next forty minutes with yachties calling in to describe, verify, and amplify details.

---

*Staphylococcal Infections. Treatment. Management
includes abscess drainage....*

—- *The Merck Manual*, Sixteenth Edition

*Day eleven
November 20, 1982
Ninety miles from Vava'u, Tonga*

The boils were getting bad. The first ones on my hands
had been joined by others. The former had swollen to the
size of nickels; they looked like mini-volcanoes with an
opening in the top, containing, instead of lava, pus and sick-
looking blood. Beneath that they were hard, sore, sensitive.

"Margaret, let me have the sewing needle, please."

"What are you going to do, Dad?"

"I'm gonna relieve the pressure on some of these. You
might do that, too." Chris had as many of the staph
infections as I did. I had one on each knuckle, two largish
ones on the back of my right hand, three on each of my
elbows, too many to count on my butt. Margaret had some
on her hands and who knew how many on her legs.

With the eye-end of the big, curved needle, I poked into
the head of the boil on the back of my hand, near the heel.
There was a membrane of skin in the mouth of the thing.
When I touched it, it hurt all the way down to the surface and
below. I pushed the dull end in, hoping it would burst, but it
didn't. I turned the needle around and pressed the point into
the center of the protuberance, but it gave fleshily, not
breaking. My stomach turned at the thought of pushing the

metal into my body. A coppery taste rose in my mouth. I scraped the point across the membrane, then did it again. I'd have to gouge the thing, not baby it. It was too tough for that. My scrotum contracted as I dug down and twisted; it broke. Pus and dark blood spurted out onto the back of my hand.

The boil hurt but the surrounding area got instant relief from the break in pressure. I pushed the dull end of the needle around and tried to scoop up more liquid. A bit came out clinging to the eye, in a sickly string. An odor rose: putrescence. I dug back in, my scrotum clenching again as I did. I got more out, a little. The hard mass beneath was unyielding. I got a bit more out, tried squeezing the top; that didn't do anything at all.

I rinsed it over the side. Then I began on the second one.

———————

Late afternoon and we were singing. We'd done some religious songs we all knew, what we call Kingdom songs. Now we were doing a Hit Parade that spanned three generations. My era was the fifties, and I didn't get much respect from the others when I'd say, "And then there was this one...", then sing, "How Much Is that Dog-gie in the Wind-owww? The one with the wag-ga-ly tail." Soon, I tried to stay with the more dignified ones, like "The Old Lamplighter." Margaret's era was the late sixties and the seventies, so from her we got a lot of Beatles. Then Chris would do a Kool and the Gang song, and some Billy Joel, which I rather liked.

Margaret, incidentally, sang off-key. But she had a captive audience.

We were capsized again in the middle of this. You never got used to it. One second you were in some state of normality, the boat beneath you, your possessions tied down around you, the wind blowing you forward toward safety; then you'd be lifted, adrenaline shooting into your bloodstream, fear in your mouth, limbs flailing for balance. You'd go under, thinking instantly of sharks, of getting separated as the current pulled directly on your body, of being swept away as you continued to be drawn along with the frightening might of the sea, down into the troughs, up the other side, needing to find the boats, needing to reach a lifeline, not knowing if the others were making it back.

We lost the sextant in its box; we'd been using it as a seat. We lost my larger pocket knife which had been in the survival stores. We lost the last remaining shoe which we'd been using to bail water.

It wasn't much before sundown when we got reorganized, the masts reset, the dinghies relashed. The jackets hanging from the masts were soaked. We put them back on again. It's a miserable feeling. The sun went down, taking with it its warmth.

---

*Starvation: Inanition. Most systems are affected....
Heart size and output are reduced. There is bradycardia
and lowered systolic, diastolic, and venous pressure.
Respiratory rate, minute volume, and vital capacity are
all reduced. The main endocrine disturbance is gonadal
atrophy with loss of libido....*

— *The Merck Manual*, Sixteenth Edition

Late that night, I lost the second oar. I'd been dozing, and I shouldn't have been. Usually I had a sort of insomnia at night and was up for most of it. My weariness was growing daily, though, and I simply dozed off. The oar slipped out of my hand and I didn't know it. I jerked awake at some point, stared stupidly at my empty hand, looked about us, and saw no sign of it. I woke Chris.

"I lost the oar," I said quietly.

"I'll get the other one," he said. He climbed forward to the Sandpiper and unstrapped our last oar. Bringing it back, he remarked, "I don't know why we didn't think of this before: Let's make a tie line for it, something we can strap to our wrists when we're steering."

"I guess we didn't think of it because we didn't have to," I muttered, reaching back to the duffel in the other boat, taking my smaller pocket knife out of the duffel. I always have pocket knives in different places. I started to cut a groove in the new tiller where we could wrap and tie a line. It would take a while.

Midnight
Colin Busch home
Kawa Kawa, Bay of Islands
New Zealand

"Colin," Janice asked, "nothing new tonight on the radio about the *Vamonos*?"

They were undressing for bed. Colin sat on the mattress with one shoe off and the second still in his hand.

"No. Nothing new. But what there was before seems to look worse with every passing day. It doesn't feel like a... benign situation, where nothing's really wrong, where your fears are just fancies — where it comes out all right and you laugh at yourself for getting so worried when there was a logical explanation."

"But when you can't be sure something's wrong, that's the agony of it, do you see? No burning house with a woman screaming 'Save my baby!' That you'd rush right into."

"And all the other people involved — nobody is sure. And you can't be the one who says, 'I'm certain. I know the house is on fire.'"

"Of course I see, Colin. And I see what it's starting to do to you. I wish I could just see what's the best thing to do."

"The only decision I've made, at this point in time, is that when Dave arrives that'll be the deadline. But I see that that's a decision — to wait. I won't be going to work tomorrow."

"You won't? Why?"

"Tomorrow I go to Auckland Search and Rescue."

Vamonos **sailing from Raiatea to Bora Bora**

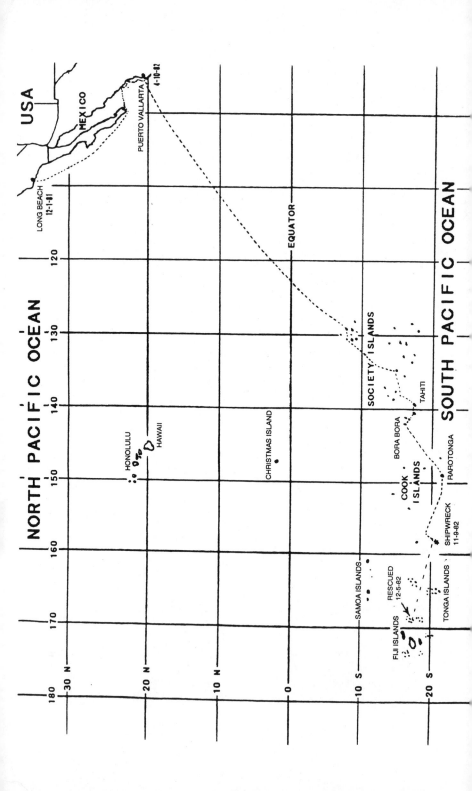

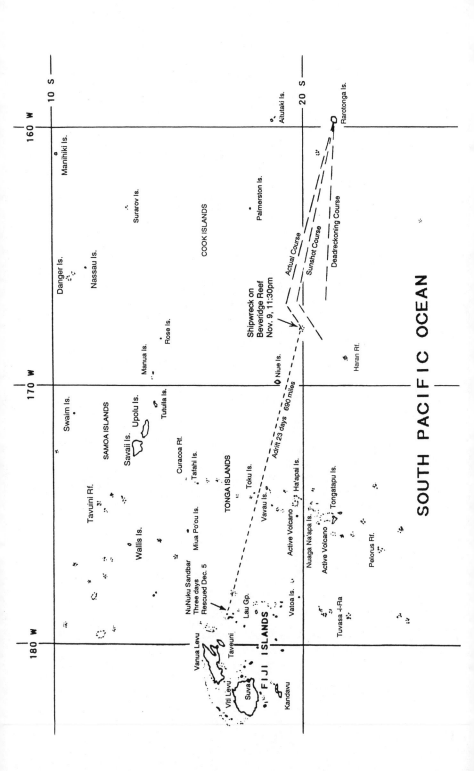

Avitua Harbor, Rarotonga three days before shipwreck

Reef and sandbar that Aroses landed on after twenty three days adrift

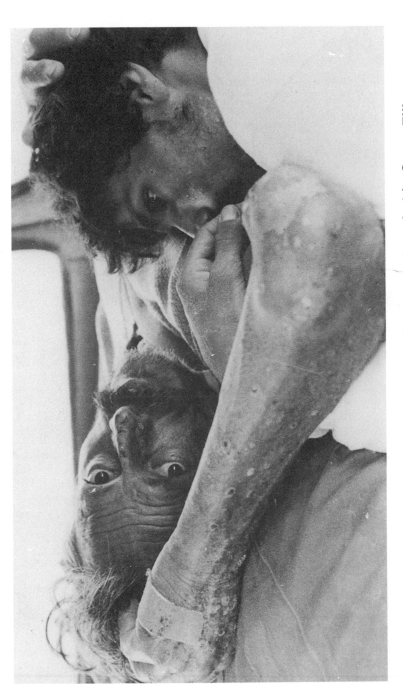

Bob and Christian in the rescue helicopter at hospital in Suva, Fiji

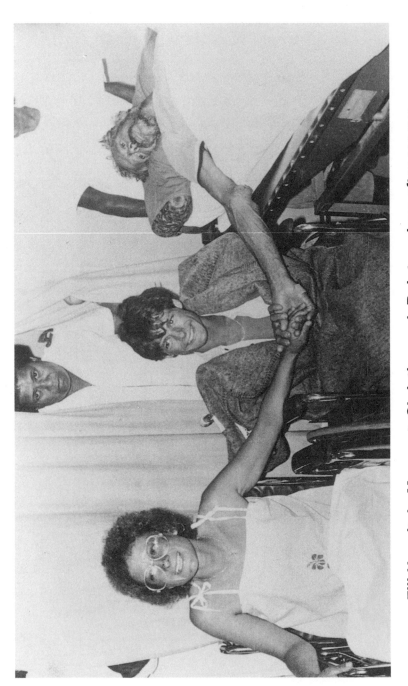

Fiji Hospital - Margaret, Christian and Bob two days after rescue

Bob Aros, Fiji nurse, helicopter pilot

Fiji nurse, Margaret Aros

Rescue helicopter pilot, Christian Aros

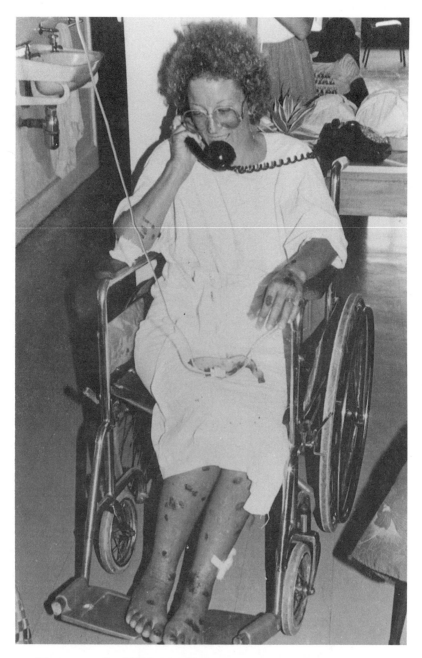

Margaret in Fiji hospital - two days after rescue

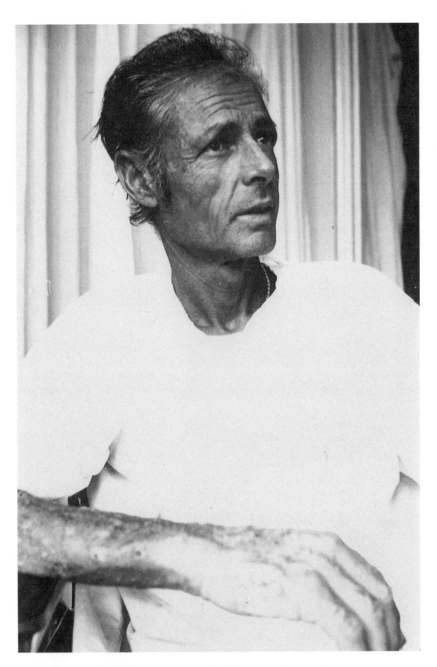

Bob Aros in Fiji hospital - Three days after rescue

Bob, Chris and Margaret in Fiji, five weeks after rescue

TWELVE

Once we finished breakfast, we had five cans of vegetables left, plus four packets of the dried food.

We'd figured on eighteen days worth of water. That looked about right. Margaret's catch during the squall had added a little, too. Maybe we had another week's supply. Another week! How could we go another week? We'd been almost two weeks adrift already! Thank God I'd been in good physical shape when we started. I've always been athletic, swimming, skiing, mountain-climbing. But now I felt so tired all the time. My body had always done whatever I'd asked it to. Now it didn't want to do much more than lie down and rest.

We had this World War II army surplus "water maker"

which we'd stowed in the survival supplies. A solar still. Made sense, didn't it? Only trouble was, when we'd tried to use it, it hadn't done us any good. It looked like a beach ball, with a flotation area, inflatable, and a bottom weight to keep it upright. The idea is that you'd put it over the side on a line, sea water would be let into the bottom part and the sun's heat would evaporate it up through a chamber. There, in a shaded section, it would cool and condense: water without salt. The previous time we'd used it, the day had been overcast and the sun probably hadn't been able to do its work. Today, it was finally sunnier, so we put it out again.

Chris and I decided to patch the Avon over its slow leak. We were pumping it twice daily now, at daybreak and sunset, because the sea buffeted it so much. A bigger patch over the old one might help. From the dinghy's patch kit, we got out a large patch and the adhesive. The right way to do the job is to deflate the craft first, but of course there was no way to do that. We dried, then roughed the area with a little rasp from the kit, spread the adhesive liberally, and pressed on the patch. Then I held it down, for an hour. The puncture was at the stern of the Avon, where it was lashed to the Sandpiper, so not too much water splashed onto it. I figured an hour was a long time, but with all the moisture around and the fact that a little air was constantly leaking from below, it was better to overdo it.

"Chris, I'll tell you what: Why don't you take over now and hold this down for, say, another three-quarters of an hour?"

"It's probably done, Dad."

"Yeah, I know, but did you have another pressing engagement?"

"Very funny, Dad. Okay, let me get my hand under yours."

He actually went a full hour with it, saying that since I'd done an hour, he would. When he finally eased off, the patch looked good. Then it very, very slowly started to bubble in the middle. I knew it was just a matter of time before the air worked the patch up so it could find a way out.

I looked at Chris. "You'd think that in this day of sending men to the moon, they could invent a patch kit that works."

———————

9:30 a.m.
Search and Rescue Headquarters
Office of the Coordinator
Auckland, New Zealand

Colin Busch walked down the nondescript hallway of the office building, past wooden doors with pebbled glass panes bearing names of shipping firms and insurance carriers, import-exporters, and the local office for the meat packers union. The corridor was airless, the day hot, and some scattered murmuring only emphasized the overall quiet. Finding the right door, he opened it and stepped in. Two men sat at desks in the single room. A third desk was uncluttered, clearly disused.

"Mr. Busch?" said the older man, pleasantly. He was about fifty, Colin reckoned, intelligent face, thinning hair, in shirtsleeves.

When Colin affirmed his identity, the man said, "My name's Miller, I'm Coordinator, and this is Captain Hillary." Miller gestured to a chair. "So, how may I help you?"

Colin started at the beginning, explaining the schedule of the Pacific Maritime Net and the incidents since November ninth. Miller listened attentively, nodding encouragingly, and took some notes. The other man, ruggedly handsome except for too-pale blue eyes, listened absently, occasionally perusing something on the desk. Colin embroidered nothing. When he'd finished, he silently waited for a response.

"I take it," began Miller, "that you're inquiring about the possibility of a search. As you probably know, Mr. Busch, New Zealand has no Coast Guard. I imagine if this were the United States, one could ring up the Guard there and they'd merely alter some of their routines and try to locate your friends somewhere out from their intended port-of-call on the usual routes. But we have no options of that sort. We do have some options, though; that's why I've asked Captain Hillary to step along from his office for this meeting. He's my maritime advisor."

"Your maritime advisor? What does that mean?"

"You see, I'm the *Coordinator* of Search and Rescue. For the Auckland area. I coordinate our efforts through the use of advisors. In a case calling for say, Air Force involvement, I have an Air Force advisor. I have a weather advisor who's with the Weather Office people, if I need someone to plot drifts or weather patterns. So, for this case, I have a maritime advisor."

"And my response to your report," put in Hillary, "is that it's much too soon to tell what's happened with these people."

"Look, mate. If I didn't think now was the time for action, I wouldn't have come yet. Things have to be started now and here should be the place for it. Is this Search and Rescue or isn't it?"

Miller said, with a friendly manner, "Again, this is Search and Rescue *Coordination* Mr. Busch. We don't scramble a squadron of helicopters standing in readiness on the roof. But I can tell you this: The procedure in a case of this sort is for the New Zealand police to take the first action. First it must be established that a supposedly missing vessel isn't quietly tied up at some little wharf somewhere nearby before we head any manpower out to sea. Once they've done their investigation, and they're very good at it too, they pass it to us and we take it from there."

With deliberate calm, Colin said, "You don't understand yachties. If Margaret and Bob had sailed all these days without being able to check in, and knowing very well that they were expected to and that people would be concerned, the first thing, the very first thing they'd do when they reached any port would be to telephone the network land base and say, `Hey, we're okay. Radio went out, fellas. Sorry for the worries.' That's guaranteed. A land search is just a waste of time."

"As you say, I may not know yachties as well as you, but I, in fact, have an advisor in the yachting community, and I will call him."

Hillary spoke again. "Procedure must be followed."

Colin took a deep breath and looked back at Miller. "I'm sure you can use your judgment in an individual case."

Miller looked thoughtfully at Colin for a moment, then turned to Hillary. "What else could we do, Captain? This gentleman is clearly genuinely concerned about his friends."

"Mr. Busch," Hillary began, "certain conditions do warrant an immediate full-scale search. These, though, do not obtain here. A distress signal from a portable device, such as an epirb, would be one. A radioed Mayday would be another. A flare or any visual sighting would certainly be another. Finally, if they were overdue, and then some. In these cases, we'd immediately plot a position if a commercial flight had picked up an epirb signal, or else we'd estimate one, then get drift information from the Weather Office and get Air Force planes out, or even one or two of our few navy ships. But here," he spread his upturned hands, "we have no such justification. In fact, we merely have a boat that is not even yet overdue. All that's out of the ordinary is that some check-ins have not been made. And, as you probably well know, an amateur radio is the most unreliable piece of equipment on a private yacht. I'm sure I don't have to tell you that, Mr. Busch."

Colin was silent for a moment. Then he said quietly, "I want you to put up a plane."

Hillary's eyes opened a bit and he said, "Haven't you heard what I've been saying?"

"Listen to what *I'm* saying. This is no time to be larking about with procedure and needing *corpus delecti* before you can act. I want you to put up a plane."

Miller spoke up, now. "Let me explain something, Mr. Busch. To put up one of the Air Force's Orion aircraft for a special search costs between seven and eight thousand dollars an hour. For this I don't need any advisors. This my office knows. The Air Force has four Orions and they're in use watching for poachers at the fisheries or suspected smuggling operations. Even then, due to the economic climate, our pilots get very little flying time even to perform these duties. Between seven and eight thousand dollars per hour, Mr. Busch."

"Just a minute, now. That's quite a figure, and I'm not disputing it, mind you, but if they have to be up there anyway to watch for poachers or whatever, then to add in possible areas where these people might be drifting isn't costing the government the whole price tag. This would just be altering their flight plans. Maybe fewer fisheries would be visited, but that's about it."

"It's not the cost to the government, really, Mr. Busch, it's the cost to the taxpayers."

"And an air rescue mission hits the newspapers."

"That's right. It hits the newspapers. I'm afraid that's the harsh reality of it. And people want to know that their money isn't being spent frivolously, aircraft going out willy-nilly. The decision has to be well grounded."

"Well grounded," Hillary put in. "As in the guidelines."

There was nothing for it. Miller, at least, was listening to him, but the other one was his expert in these matters. The system was obviously designed so that he'd make use of the expert's opinion.

"Listen," said Colin quietly. "How about this... If the Air Force have any flights out looking for anything at all, could they please look for this particular yacht? I've a picture here and a full description. It's easily identified by blue covers and the name is clear on the side."

Hillary shuffled some papers on his desk.

Colin went on, "If they'll just do a low pass on any yacht coming into New Zealand just to identify it, perhaps they'll come back and say to us, 'It's okay. The boat's on it's way in, only a hundred or so miles off shore'."

After a moment, Miller said, "I'll be glad to arrange that much, Mr. Busch. Let me have the picture."

We were drinking the afternoon water. We would rotate who went first. Seems silly, but we'd get so thirsty, going first was that much better than going second. Margaret took her drink, careful at the end to be leaving two-thirds. Chris drank next, then handed me the can.

We capsized. Under water, I held onto the can. I'd get my drink from the solar still.

Once we'd righted the dinghies and climbed on board, I looked at the tangle of lines among the windsurfer, the trailing sock, and the water maker. I hauled in the still and saw that the upper portion was awash with sea water. There'd been a couple of ounces of fresh water in there last time I'd looked.

I threw the can over the side.

After sundown, the clouds parted, and we looked up at a waning moon.

Margaret said, "Someone is sitting, safe and warm somewhere, looking up at this same moon. It's amazing, at this very instant, they're looking, thinking — what? About others doing the same thing, maybe? Not that there might be others adrift at sea looking at it, but thinking something. It gives you a feeling of connectedness. With everyone on the planet."

"Maybe someone is thinking there could be someone adrift on this ocean," Chris said.

"Well," she said, "If we ever get back to a place safe and warm, if we ever get home, I'm going to make it a point to, every once in a while, look up at the moon and send my heart out to someone who might be lost at sea."

10:30 p.m.
Colin Busch home
Kawa Kawa, Bay of Islands
New Zealand

"...All right then, Harry. Sounds like you should make port here real soon. Now let me ask you: Have you seen any aircraft making a low pass at you today? Would've had to come down pretty close, close enough to read your boat's name. Zebra Lima *** Bravo Kilo Delta standing by."

"This is Sierra Romeo *** Romeo Charlie India. No, Colin, not a thing. I heard the others answer that they hadn't seen anything, either, and I was thinking — You said they were Orions. Well, these Orions are really quiet. The engines are designed to be quiet. And, there's this besides — they can cruise on just two of their four engines, you know, to double their range. That makes 'em even quieter. So maybe there were some passes when people were belowdecks and didn't notice 'em. Could be. Sierra Romeo *** Romeo Charlie India standing by."

"This is Zebra Lima *** Bravo Kilo Delta. Yeah, Harry. Well, thanks for that. Could be."

———————

The night was black. I had the tiller, had had it for a couple of hours. My bottom hurt like crazy. I was sitting on a lifejacket to keep above the water in the boat, but I could feel every seam of the thing on my butt amid a wash of low-grade pain. My legs and bare feet had developed their share of boils, too. I'd tried not to move my legs under the cover, because I didn't want to disturb Margaret's restless sleep, but now I was going to have to. One of my legs was stretched between her and the gunwale, the other leg's shin was under her. I started to pull back the latter, gritting my teeth, when from under the cover came, "Oh! Ow!"

"I've got to move my leg," I whispered.

"No, don't — let me move my arm first..."

"Ahh! You hit my leg!"

"Ouch!," from Chris, awake now.

"I'm sorry, Chris," she said.

I yelled, "Chris! Don't rub your arm against mine!"

"Wait everybody," from Margaret. "Just move easy, take it slow... ooo!"

"Okay, Margaret," I said. "I'm lifting my left leg."

"Okay..."

"I'm gonna cross it over to my right, okay?"

"Wait, Margaret!" from Chris. "Don't roll on — oh!"

I got my leg moved. I could hear the two of them panting lightly as they tried to settle back to sleep.

———————————

Day thirteen
November 22, 1982
Thirty nautical miles from Vava'u, Tonga

"I think we passed Tonga," I announced. "Even at one knot, we should have reached something by now. We must have passed right through — maybe in the night, when we couldn't see." I didn't want to admit it. We'd been going so long, thinking: Tonga, soon we'll hit Tonga. But I was weary of it, too. All right. That was that, then.

I spread the chart on my knees. I had to be delicate with the thing. It was always wet like everything else, always ready to rip. Time to look at what we could do, now. Well, more like what was open to us now. Boy, I'd really taken charge that first day. "It's like any other voyage," I'd said. "And Tonga is just our next port of call." Yeah. I'd been in control of the boats and the sea and our future. Now what? After the thin, north-south line that was the Tongan group, open sea stretched until Fiji. I measured it on the chart. From a little past Tonga to the nearest Fiji group, the Exploring Islands, was about 300 miles. Three hundred miles.

From Beveridge or Haran Reef, whichever one we had hit, we'd come about 400 miles. We'd been adrift thirteen days. That meant about thirty nautical miles a day. So 300 more would take ten more days. If my figuring was correct. Was I completely wrong about where we were and the direction we were being taken?

I told the others what I'd come up with. There was a pause.

"Okay, Dad. You'll get us out of this."

"If only I'd grabbed more food — and the juice, maybe — we'd be able to last no matter how far we had to go — "

"Margaret," Chris said. "You cut that out." Sometimes he simply amazed me. "We thought we would hit Tonga and you got us enough supplies to get us here, and we still have more."

I used my heartiest voice and said, "On to Fiji!!"

"Next stop, Fiji!" yelled Chris.

————————————

Colin Busch office
Kawa Kawa Post Office
Bay of Islands
New Zealand

"Colin. Phone for you. Line two."

Colin put down his work and picked up the receiver, identifying himself.

This is Search and Rescue, Wellington, Mr. Busch. My name is Daniels."

"Search and Rescue, Wellington? I spoke to Search and Rescue, Auckland — a Mr. Miller and a fella named Hillary."

"I know Miller, of course. Is he taking care of the *Vamonos* situation?"

"No, no. Not really. What can I do for you, Mr. Daniels?"

"Well, your associate on your maritime radio network has apparently been talking with my counterpart at Search and Rescue in Sydney, Australia."

"Oh. That'd be Bruce."

"All right. In any case, we have his report to them, and they called us because this area of the ocean is in New Zealand's jurisdiction. Now, it seems to us serious enough that we'd like to be put into the picture by you, since your associate said he didn't think you'd mind if he gave us your name."

"Quite right, perfectly okay. Where shall I start?"

"We understand they were keeping regular scheds on your net, and then you lost contact abruptly. Do you have their last position? And I understand there was a course change?"

"I have my log with me. Hold the line, would you?"

For the next twenty minutes, Colin gave nautical information, the insights he had into the *Vamonos*'s seaworthiness, the viewpoint a maritime mobile unit would have if deprived of their transmission capability, and the proximity of the sloop, *Karana*, to New Zealand.

He continued, "Now if we can backtrack a bit, Mr. Daniels, their last position, as I said, was northeast of both Beveridge and Haran Reefs. They would have had to correct pretty drastically to the southwest to get back on a heading to New Zealand. If you plot this, as I have, you'll see that that'd put them on a course to pass just west of the reefs. It's come to my attention that at least two published nautical charts show these reefs in different positions." There was silence on the other end of the line. "Things happen at sea, Mr. Daniels."

"I thank you for all your information, Mr. Busch. May I call you in future, if need be?"

"Would that be in the near future, Mr. Daniels?"

"I understand your concern, sir. I can only promise that, since these things take a certain amount of time, I won't be wasting any."

"I can't tell you how glad I am to hear that."

————————

"Sooty Shearwater (puffinus griseus)... inhabit the southern Pacific in the antipodean summer, nesting in burrows which they dig on small islands off New Zealand (three million pairs on the Snares), Tasmania, the Falklands and Chile. In the southern autumn they make a long migration across the equator to enjoy the northern summer as far north as temperate coasts off North America, Japan and the North Atlantic."

— Eric Hosking and Ronald M. Lockley
Seabirds of the World

Where do those little birds come from? I wondered. I'd always thought that the presence of birds meant proximity to land, but there they are, day after day, totally at home, scores of them. About the size of sparrows, always scanning the water for food, dapping, then flapping on. I guess they eat algae. I never see them catch any tiny fish. They land on the water and float like ducks, random clusters of them. The ocean is always moving, but they know the movements. They take off, skimming just inches above the surface, up with the swells, down into the troughs, through them and across them. They seem totally at ease. Unafraid of anything. They won't come near us, of course. Why should they? We're just driftwood in their little bird world. Just passing through. Wouldn't make much of a meal, a bird that small. I'd eat them, though. Skin one and eat it. Catch another one. Skin it and eat it, too.

———————————

Late that afternoon, we were capsized. As I pulled myself up on the overturned Avon, I saw that three tiny sea urchins had attached themselves to the bottom. I scraped them off with my fingernails and swallowed them.

THIRTEEN

Day fourteen
November 23, 1982
Nearing the gap between Vava'u and
Toku Islands, Tonga

"It is enough to strike the row of puko trees..."

— Tuita navigator proverb

I'd been lifting myself up on my hands to look for land before the sun went down. Past Tonga or not, I was still going to keep up the surveillance. I did that five or six times a day, sometimes more. Once I finished, my eye caught Margaret looking at me strangely. "What?" I asked.

"It's just — your cheeks are getting so hollow."

"Yeah, well, I've been on a diet." As I said it, I could hear the weakness in my voice. More vigorously I said, "You've gotten nice and trim, yourself."

"Oh, Bob, stop joking. I'm worried about you. You've always been thin, you didn't have anything extra on you. Even your eyes seem to be standing out more than they did... And your beard, all that gray — Bob, you weren't that gray."

"I'm all right, Margaret. Too little sleep and too much strain, that's all."

"Bob, I'm not watching you die, am I?"

"What a silly thing to say. Nobody's gonna die."

At nine p.m., Chris woke me and asked me to take the helm. My wrist watch's numbers glowed in the gloom surrounding us. Nine o'clock, just like the beginning of Margaret's last watch on the *Vamonos*.

Around ten, the sea became peculiar. The swells lessened and the current picked up. We began moving faster and faster on a flatter sea. Chop developed — short, broken wave movement. I worked the oar rapidly and with increasing variety, trying to keep us in line with the current. There was white water all around.

"Chris," I whispered, "are you awake?" Apparently not. I called quietly to Margaret's form under the cover, but she didn't answer. There didn't seem to be any immediate danger, but this was so peculiar, they might like to see it.

It was like riding the rapids on a mountain river. I became

engrossed in steering. It was very exciting. The dinghies really responded to the rudder, just like in a shallow river bed — that's what makes rapids: A deep river, flowing along, suddenly gets shallow and the water is rushed over the reduced area, roiling with the force following it.

I was on the starboard side, because I had the oar. We'd start to veer. I'd shift the tiller and it'd come right over. Veer, shift, swing, compensate, wind in my hair, flat sea — what a difference from the implacable swelling and just trying to keep the dinghies right side up!

After maybe an hour and a half, the chop began to lessen, the white water to fall off, and the swells to increase. The sea picked up and finally resumed its former manner. Then, strangely, it continued to rise, higher than the normal night sea, higher and higher until we were in giant swells, thirty footers, sea such as we'd never seen when it wasn't the shank of the afternoon. I was back to the constant rudder, to the watch for rogues, to the fear of capsizing in the dark, always more terrifying than going under in the daylight.

Eventually, exhausted, I woke Chris and handed back the helm.

Day fifteen
November 24, 1982
Twelve miles past Vava'u, Tonga

Maybe there isn't a search party out for us. Maybe we're going to actually die. I wonder if the others think that, too. I'm certainly not going to mention it. I'm supposed to be the strong one.

I don't feel strong. I feel so tired all the time. I feel so hungry. What would starvation feel like? Do you get past the point of hunger? We have two cans of vegetables left, and the packets of dried food. Then I'll start to find out what it's like.

Margaret was catnapping this late morning when Chris said to me in a low mutter, "I've seen some fins, maybe shark fins. Have you?" A little jolt of fear went through me. He'd touched on something that was always in the back of my mind. My reply was equally quiet.

"Yes, at least I think they were shark. I've definitely seen fins."

"How many times?"

"Half a dozen," I said. "Maybe eight."

"Me, about eight or nine." He paused. "Let's not tell Margaret."

"No," I agreed. "Let's not."

We talked about food again for a while, the Caribbean cruise we'd been on with its buffets, and elaborate scheduled meals and cocktail hour hors d'oeuvres. Somehow, remembering the abundance made it a little easier to deal with our deprivation.

It was late afternoon and the swells were at fifteen feet.

My ability to concentrate on the conversation dwindled as my nervousness about the swells increased. In the first days, they didn't get to me at all. Ten feet, fifteen feet, twenty, no matter. But I was so weak. I seemed covered with boils. I had nothing like strength; I was always tired. Let me just stay here, not be flung out of my boat, not be swallowed by the sea. We capsized.

I hit the water and plunged deep into its heaviness. Cold. Not again. Too much, too much. I squeezed my eyes tightly shut. My chest hurt. I kicked my legs a little. The air inside my lungs bore me to the surface.

I opened my eyes. The raft, the lifeline right there. I put out my hand and grabbed it, thinking: Holding on again. Holding onto a dinghy in the middle of the Pacific. I could let go. I heard Chris and Margaret calling out to me from the other side. I could let go and drift away. It'll be all over.

"Bob! Are you there?"

Drift away. Not be afraid every day. Not try to do the impossible.

"Bob! Where are you??"

"Dad! Maybe he's under the boat, hit his head — I'm going under —"

"I'm here," I croaked. "I'm all right."

The solar still was torn up beyond repair. Big deal. But we'd lost the pump for the Avon. Its tie line hadn't held through the capsizing. The soft dinghy needed to be pumped up. We always did it around this time.

"Can we blow it up ourselves?" asked Margaret.

The valve housing was about two inches in diameter. Chris craned his head down to it, about four inches above the floor of the dinghy, put his lips around it and blew. "Yeah," he said. "I can blow hard enough to move the valve." He continued to blow into it for about a minute. "Phew. Gotta rest."

"I'll try it," said Margaret. Trading places with Chris, she worked on it for a bit. When she stopped, her face was red from the exertion. Even blowing up balloons takes a lot of pressure. This was a valve designed for a mechanical pump. They traded back and forth for about fifteen minutes. By then the gunwale was pretty well inflated.

Both Margaret and I were sleeping restlessly when I heard Chris yell, "Ouch!! Margaret! My ankle!"

Under the cover, she shifted. I yelled, "Ow. No, not that way!" and jerked my boil-ridden calf away.

"Oh! Wait, ow!" she cried.

"Ow!" screeched Chris.

A couple of seconds went by, then from under the cover came a giggle. Chris cracked up.

"I chortled. "Ouch, ooo, ouch, ooo, yow!"

———————————

Day sixteen
November 25, 1982

Fruit cocktail. The second to last can, and we'd come full circle to fruit cocktail again. You never knew what you'd get from these labelless cans.

Share the water. About ten cans left. Nine after this one. We'll run out about day twenty if we don't find land. A little longer than I figured; must have been a bit more than four and a half gallons to start.

The boils. Gotta shift position. Ugh, ooh. Okay. That's not bad. Yes, that's all right.

In the survival movies and books, there always comes a time when they're starving to death, water gone too. So we would still live for a while, live like that. So how many days would that be? Food runs out tomorrow — no, wait, we have those dried food packets. But we'll need to use water on them to make them edible, use up drinking water. Well, say the food and water both run out on day twenty.

So how long?... Twenty-nine days, say. That's how long we could last, no food, no water. Yeah, twenty-nine days. Then we'd die.

Uh! My leg is killing me. And my butt. Gotta shift. Okay. Better.

Should scrape the boils again. Do that in a few minutes. Chris is in the hard dinghy? How can he stand that? Mustn't be sitting. Probably crouched, the way he does, like an Aborigine. I can't balance like that. I'm not up to going forward any more. Precarious. Margaret doesn't go forward, either.

But to go twenty-nine days, we'd have to not get capsized

again. We'd be too weak. We couldn't climb back into the dinghies. Or not all of us would get back. I wouldn't; I'd die. Oh, Jehovah, please give me the strength and the courage to fight and stay alive. If not please resurrect me. Margaret might last. She seems all right, still strong. Women have an extra layer of fat, maybe that's helping.

Chris has been so washed out these last couple of days. He does boat work, takes his turns at the oar, but he's really unhappy. He won't do Steve Martin anymore. He's the physically strongest of the three, I think, but it's just his mental state. Margaret said to him this morning, "So, Chris, still longing for that ice cream? Any particular flavor?" and he'd said, "Not ice cream. What I'd really like is a bowl of warm water. With maybe a little steam coming off the top. And some bread in it. Bread soup." We got so chilled at night. I could understand it.

I don't know if, with food and water gone, he'd get through many capsizings. We're never going to get rescued. I don't know what happened, but we're out here on our own.

If they were looking, they'd've found us by now.

11:30 p.m.
On the road from Opua Harbor
Bay of Islands, New Zealand

"You know, Colin, the last time we drove anywhere, Bob was doing the driving in a beat-up old van," said Dave.

Turning to his wife, he said, "It's funny, isn't it, Jan?"

"And they gave us all that fresh fruit the day they left," she said from the back seat. "I keep imagining them out there somewhere on a raft every time I eat a piece of fruit."

"We've all been thinking of them, Jan. I met the *Windtree* this morning and collected Harry and Nancy — You should have seen them. Not at all like people on a pleasure cruise. Very subdued. They're staying with us. They're at the house now."

They drove a bit in silence. Then Dave said, "No one can be sure they're in trouble, but what's your gut-feeling, Colin?"

"My intuition, if you will, is that something is very wrong."

Jan said, "That's what I think, too. Or feel."

"Y'know," said Colin, feeling it should be said, "they could have stopped off somewhere."

"No," Jan stated firmly. "They wouldn't do that. Not without telling us."

"The authorities must be used to dealing with these situations," said Dave. "They should know how to assess them. How come they're so sure that everything's okay?"

"They're not sure everything's okay. Their point is that they're also not sure that anything's wrong. They have a costly decision to make in these cases and they want to be sure they're doing the right thing." Colin made a turn onto a small, quiet street with a high metal antenna-tower rising above one of the houses. "Well, that sounds good on the face of it, but when you take another look at that, *no* one could be sure at this point — they're not gonna suddenly put up a flare when they haven't before." He pulled into the driveway of the house fronting the tower. "We have to use some bloody common sense."

Once in the house, Dave and Jan met Janice Busch and greeted fellow yachties Harry and Nancy. Janice suggested coffee, turning down offers of assistance, and the others settled down in the living room.

Colin said, "I'm the one, perhaps, with the fullest picture of the various events here, so why don't I go over what we're looking at." He took them through the series of events, with the others occasionally asking questions or filling in bits. Janice returned with a tray of coffee things and two large plates of sticky buns. Sitting, she heard her husband say, "Finally, today, I had some people come back on the radio saying that they'd previously done one or two phone patches for Bob and Margaret to numbers in the States, and now they've received one or two inquiries: had they heard from the *Vamonos*, that sort of thing. Naturally, they said no, they hadn't but that perhaps conditions hadn't been good. They certainly didn't tell anybody we feel they're overdue."

"But we do," said Jan.

"I dunno if we all do. Do we?" asked Colin, looking round at their faces.

"Nancy and I certainly do," said Harry.

"We couldn't have got here before them," said Dave. "Even if they got too far north just out of Rarotonga and even if they had to motor on three cylinders. No, they should have been here already."

"We're agreed, then," said Colin. "Now, what should we do?"

"Maybe some of the trouble we're having," his wife ventured, "is due to none of us being related to them. An irate brother or sister pounding at the door might get the authorities into action a bit quicker. I know it would me."

"There may be something in that, luv," said Colin. "And, if that's the thing we need, perhaps we have a way to get it. Those phone patches, or at least one of them, may have been to a relative."

"Do you have their phone numbers?"

"I didn't talk to these land units on the phone, I talked to them on the radio. I have their call-signs in my log."

"I think this is a good idea," said Harry. "I think we should get on to them."

"Right. I'll do that now, if I can, if they're by their sets."

He left them for a few minutes while they talked among themselves, drinking coffee and eating some of the buns. There were still quite a few buns left on the plates when Colin returned and sat.

"None of them up at the moment. It's a bit late. I'll try again first thing in the morning. I'll also ask if there's anyone else out there who may have done a phone patch. Have you come up with anything else?"

Harry said, "Only that it's about time we got a search going."

Day seventeen
November 26, 1982

In the dark before dawn, the sea began to swell. This was the second time it did this in the morning. What was going on? As soon as the sky lightened a little, I twisted around to see if we were approaching landfall. Nothing in front. Nothing half left. Nothing full left. Nothing to starboard at all.

I kept the dinghies square to the following swells. They reached ten feet. The motion woke Chris. "What is it?"

"I don't know, son. It started about ten minutes ago."

"Is it land?"

"I looked and didn't see any. Look again."

Margaret's fingers were undoing the ties on the cover from underneath.   She got one side loose and pushed herself up on her elbow. "What's happening?"

"I don't know," I said. "Just high seas, probably." She undid all the forward part of the cover and rolled it up behind her, then leaned on it. "Don't you want to let that dry as much as it can?" I asked her.

"Not in these seas," she said. Smart.

"I don't see anything, Dad."

"Neither did I." The swells were at fifteen feet, now. Fifteen up, fifteen back to sea level, fifteen into the trough. Thirty from trough to crest. Amazing — it was dawn, not the middle of the afternoon. The wind was blowing hard.

"Should we eat in all this?" Margaret asked me.

"I'm hungry," Chris put in.

"Yes, all right," I said. "Should be fine. Chris, take over."

I reached behind me into the hard dinghy. Opening the mouth of the pillowcase, I put my hand in and, as I had every morning, pulled out a can of food. Only this morning it was the last can of food. I opened it.

Peas. We enjoyed them.

We passed around our pint of water. "Tomorrow," I said, "we'll have to start on the dried food."

"That'll be a change, anyway," Chris said wryly.

"Yes," said Margaret, "but don't you see? It'll mean using some of our drinking water to make it edible. You know, `just add water'. We have about... How much, Bob?"

"About three more days' worth."

"So the dried food causes a problem."

Before, Margaret might have said this in a lecturing, mothering way. Now, it came out as consultation with Chris, consultation with an equal. He said, mildly, "You know? Maybe we should use sea water instead."

And he'd certainly grown.

Margaret said, "Chris, that's a very good idea."

If the waves were going to keep up like this, what were they going to be like in the afternoon? I'd stayed the night once at a friend's house; we'd slept in his room on the third floor; looking down from that third-floor window in the morning was like looking over the side of the dinghy now.

Except that had been safe. All across the walls of the wave and scattered across the troughs were those little birds, the only life we ever saw. Well, unless you counted the sea urchins. And those fins. Chris had the helm, and I was trying to get some rest, maybe even sleep. I imagined Polynesian natives appearing in out-riggers, could see them clearly, could picture their surprise at happening across us in the vast reaches of the ocean. To be out on the sea was natural to them; they navigated by sensing variations in the swells below their seats and by immense familiarity with the night skies. Not like us. We were here against our will. But we were dealing with it. We were still getting along.

We were flung sideways and over and I left the boat flying backwards while it fell away from me. I dropped ten feet before hitting the water sideways and going under. Not again, not again. But I didn't go so deep because of the angle at which I'd hit. Surfacing, I turned and saw the dinghies, side by side upside-down, trailing me. A few weary strokes got me back to them and, as I threw my arm over the exposed bottom of the Sandpiper, I saw Chris and then Margaret appear alongside the Avon. I saw the duffel bag floating by. It had the dried food in it. And the flares and chart. It hadn't been tied down; we'd unlashed it to inspect the food packets. Usually we didn't batten everything down until the beginning of the afternoon. I stretched out my left hand to grab it, not letting go of the Sandpiper. Couldn't reach it unless I let go. I didn't want to let go. I felt weak, battered. Had to get the duffel. Had to get the food. Maybe one of the others could reach it easier. I turned and there was Margaret, swimming away.

"Margaret! Where are you going?" I shouted, but then I saw for myself: The water jug was floating ten feet out.

"Come back," I yelled, but she kept going. The jug was getting beyond my field of vision behind me, so I turned back to the boat and twisted around the other way. I spotted her — twenty feet out. She was clutching the water container. She circled around, looked back toward me, and saw the gap of charging, cascading sea separating us. A shocked look came to her face. She stretched out and began kicking her legs, swimming, holding the jug to her chest. She didn't make any headway, though. The current was taking her farther away.

"Dad! Do you see Margaret out there?!"

"Yeah, yeah!"

"Should I get her? On the windsurfer?"

I looked back at him. Holding onto the Avon lifeline with one hand, he had the line to the windsurfer in the other. "Yes!" I yelled. "But be careful! Hurry!"

He hauled himself up onto the surfer, got to his knees, and pulled himself to the Avon, grabbing the oar from it. He undid the towline and started paddling furiously. The long white sail-sock trailed behind, foolishly. Margaret, still trying to swim, was forty feet away now. Chris stopped for a moment, pulled in the sock, and shoved it between his knees.

"Margaret!" Chris yelled, paddling again. "Keep trying to swim back!" The water jug gave her a little buoyancy. I could see her face, see the cold fear, she was cut off from us, on her own, in the middle of the ocean.

Hand over hand, I moved back along the overturned Sandpiper to get to the soft dinghy. I pulled myself up onto the bottom of it, grabbed handfuls of the far gunwale, and slid backwards, righting the thing. The Sandpiper came with it. Climbing in, panting, I turned to look for them. Where were my wife and son?

I heard Chris yelling, "Grab my hand!" I crested and saw them seventy, eighty feet away. Margaret reached up with one hand, missed his outstretched arm and, sinking, grabbed the windsurfer.

"Let go of the jug and grab my hand!" he yelled.

"Can't — " I heard her say, "lose it — Can't lose it!"

"You have to! You have to climb on!"

"Pull... Pull me..."

Her hand slipped off the surfer as the current separated them. Chris took three frantic strokes to close the gap again. Throwing the paddle between his knees, he reached down and grabbed her arm and the belt of her jeans. Twisting, he pulled her aboard. I lost sight of them as the dinghies lowered into a trough and they sank into a different one. I stared, waiting, not knowing, praying. I reached the crest of the next wave. They were a hundred feet away.

Chris was bringing them around in a half-circle, Margaret sprawled flat, facing forward, paddling with her arms. She'd thrust the water jug down her body and grabbed it between her knees. I heard Christian shout, "Paddle, Margaret! We're far! We're far!"

I knelt helplessly, watching the two people I loved most in the world. Chris, kneeling behind Margaret, digging deep into the water with the oar. Margaret paddling with her arms. Both grimly staring straight ahead.

They'll move now, I thought. They'll come back. Soon I got out of synchronization with them, could no longer see what was happening. When next I saw them, my heart jerked in my chest — they were even farther away. Chris was paddling like mad; Margaret was giving it her all. What was going on??

Chris's face filled with surprise as he saw the distance between us. He said something to Margaret, and her head jerked up. Chris shouted something at me but I couldn't make it out. He shouted again. Why weren't they making headway? I couldn't paddle to them, Chris had our last oar. I was helpless, helpless to save my family. They'd never last in these seas. I moaned, a low aching sound. They'd never —

Turn the dinghies over. I don't know where that thought came from, but... Yes, that should slow me down. I was slipping away from them faster than they could get to me!

Grabbing the port gunwale, I rolled over the starboard side, bringing both dinghies with me. Would this do any good?

Finding its lifeline, I held on and twisted around. My perspective was lower now; the waves had moved out of synch, and I couldn't see them. Come on, come on, let me see them... Should have seen them by now. Definitely should have seen them by now. *Have* to have seen them by now. They must have veered away! Where are they? Come on, more waves, align again, come on, come on — There! Over to the right — and they're closer, but going in the wrong direction! "Chris! Turn right!" He didn't hear me. His head was down, struggling to make headway. "*Chriiis-tiaan! Chriiis-tiaaaan!*" There! His head had snapped up but he still didn't see me. "*Tu-uurn staarboaaard*" He turned and saw me, changed hands with the paddle, dug in and away with the paddle, their direction changing.

"Keep going, Margaret," I heard him yell. "Keep going."

Every two strokes, he switched sides instead of using the J stroke on just one side. His arms must be very tired. Margaret had to be very near exhaustion.

We all went down into troughs.

Come on, come on, let me see... Where are they? Where are they? Come on — Yes!! They're closer! Come on, son — You're doing it, you're doing it! Could they really close the distance? Thirty-five feet. He was paddling erratically, moving the oar from his left side to his right every stroke. His arms must be dead. He croaked, "Paddle, Margaret."

I heard her moan, "Chris, I can't — anymore."

He raised his head, looked at me. Twenty-five feet.
"We're doing it, Margaret! We're doing it! Keep going!"
Come on, you're doing great! C'mon —
"You're almost here!" I yelled. Their wheezing filled the air.
"Put... out your hand... Margaret!" croaked Chris. She
lifted her head from the board and stretched out to me. I
grabbed her wrist and pulled them to the dinghy.

———————

"Thank you, Jehovah," I said, on my knees, once the
dinghies were righted. I looked at the two of them, utterly
spent, still gasping for breath. Something squeezed my
heart, seeing them in the boat again. They'd almost gone —
gone forever. I crawled to them, put my arms around them,
cried like I'd never done before. Margaret wept quietly.
Chris, crying too, rose and hugged the two of us. "Yes,"
he said, "thank you, Jehovah."
But it was critical to get the boats lined up against the
following seas. With the swells this high, we wouldn't even
need a rogue wave to be thrown right back into it. Getting
the paddle into the oarlock and its loop around my wrist, I
maneuvered us around. Chris quickly tied on the windsurfer
and its trailing sock, then tightened up the lines lashing the
two dinghies. Margaret tied down the water jug. We'd lost
the duffel. And its contents.
"Dad? Margaret? If we're going to die — I mean, if we
have to die? Let's do it together. Okay? Not separate.
Together."

I looked at him for a long moment. Then I said, "Yes. That would be best." I glanced at Margaret.

"Yes," she said. "Let's never separate again."

In the forward dinghy, alone, I worked to untangle the mess that capsizing had made of sail, guy lines, and masts. With the first mast finally free from the tangle, I started on the second. One end of the mast was in the water and I was holding the other when the mast pulled out of my grip. Into the water and gone. I stared after it into the depths.

The sea... took that, I seethed. On purpose.

"This is Victor *** Zebra Charlie calling Zebra Lima *** Bravo Kilo Delta. Standing by."

"This is Zebra Lima *** Bravo Kilo Delta standing by."

"This is Victor *** Zebra Charlie. My name is Ray Neeves, I'm a land unit in Los Angeles, California. I just came up and heard your request. I also put through some phone patches from Margaret Aros, Kilo Alpha *** Quebec India India. Those are the folks who stopped coming up about two weeks ago, right? What can I do for you?" He gave his call sign and stood by.

Colin gave his call sign and said, "I'm glad you heard me,

Ray. I'm the land base in New Zealand for the Pacific Maritime Net; perhaps you know that. In any case, we're trying to get in touch with relatives of the Aros's and hoped that the phone patch records would get us some names and numbers. Do you have records?"

"Yeah, I dug up the three numbers before I called you. Numbers but no names, I'm afraid. I don't know if these are relatives or what."

"Uh-huh. Too bad, but we can try them anyhow. Will you give those numbers a call?"

"Sure. I'll help any way I can. You're worried about these folks, huh? Okay, I'll give them all a call in the morning. See what happens."

"Uhh, if you would, I'd rather you called them now."

"Well, I was thinking it's pretty late, here. It's ten-thirty already."

"Ray, you have no idea what it's taking to get the authorities to do anything on this. Everything takes lots of time. Delaying a day on our part means a day or even two more before something gets done. And, if we're right, if they're out there, if they've been out there seventeen days, another day could make the difference. Between life and death."

"I'll call them now. Do you want to stay with me while I phone?"

"Yeah, mate. Let's go to 1560 to keep this frequency clear."

The person who answered at the first number said that the owner of the phone was away at Phoenix. The second rang and rang with no answer. The third had an answering machine. Ray left a message.

Without that sail, our forward speed would be cut in half.
The remaining mast pole was too short to cut in half again.
Nothing else in the boats could serve as a mast, so square-
rigging was out. I cut the material into the shape of a
conventional sail, a tall triangle. The nylon lines were
rotting now from the salt water, so it took some fudging and
jury-rigging to get the sail working. The single mast went
into the starboard cup-hole, supporting one side of the sail.
I punctured a hole in the bottom corner of the newly shaped
material and ran a line through it. The other end of the line
I secured to the port side of the dinghy. The wind filled the
little sail. It wasn't as good as the old one, but at least we
were sailing again.

Colin Busch home
Kawa Kawa, Bay of Islands
New Zealand
8:00 p.m. local time

"This is Victor *** Zebra Charlie calling Zebra Lima ***
Bravo Kilo Delta. Standing by..."

"This is Zebra Lima *** Bravo Kilo Delta. Colin Busch.
What's up, Ray?"

"I've been trying that no-answer number and haven't
been able to get anyone there. But I just got a phone call
from the guy who I left a message for. His name's Leonard

Smith. He's Margaret's brother. He wants a few more details from you, which we can do through me — I have him on the line now. After that he's gonna hang up and call the U.S. Coast Guard. He's gonna raise hell."

FOURTEEN

*In temperate conditions and at moderate levels of
physical activity, a person can survive on water alone
for more than two months... (survival times are
shorter in hot or cold conditions and at high
levels of activity)....*

*Water that would normally be excreted in the urine is
absorbed by the tissues. The accumulated fluid causes
edema (swelling), mainly of the legs and abdomen.*

— *American Medical Association Encyclopedia of Medicine*

Day eighteen
November 27, 1982

For the first time, there was no can of food.

I pulled yesterday's empty can to me by its string, then undid the cap of the water jug. The day before, after eating our last can of food, it finally occurred to us that it would be smart to poke a hole in this one and tie it to the boat with string. We used the sail needle to puncture it. The knives were gone. With the previous cans, just like with the oars, we'd blithely left them on the floors of the dinghies until we were down to our last, ready to be lost when we capsized. Well, we used the cans constantly for bailing, so maybe it was natural. Still, now this last one was tied on.

I poured out the morning water. Looked like about seven cans left. Two a day, then we'd be empty. I said a prayer, as usual, before we drank.

Our clothes had pretty much rotted through from the constant exposure to salt water. Holes and rips everywhere. Too bad we'd lost Chris's extra clothes. Through some of the holes in Margaret's jeans, you could see boils. Her legs look swollen inside the jeans. Her feet are definitely swollen. My own legs have plenty of these staph infections, but I take off my pants every morning and get some sun on them. And my bottom. Oh, my butt hurts. Lying on my stomach in the warm sun, when there was a warm sun, felt so good by comparison.

Chris and Margaret continue to blow up the Avon by mouth, twice a day. I'm too weak for that.

The plywood transom at the stern of the hard dinghy has fallen off. That's the place you attach the motor. Too much friction and yanking on it where they're tied, I guess. And salt water. The eyebolts that pass through it are loose, now. Still can tie the mast lines to them, though, until the holes they pass through enlarge too much.

Around three o'clock, the seas were too high for us to do much of anything but sit. Chris had the tiller but I was staring at the swells from force of habit. Regular swells, very high, as high as they got, with that pyramid action at the crest. Down into the trough as this wave passes, the next one coming on from behind, lifting us, higher, higher. At the top we just kept going, up, out of the water, back — we yelled, the Avon continued back, somersaulting, and we started to fall backwards, head first. The crest had passed and we fell almost ten feet before hitting the water. Something smacked my forehead. Down under. In my surprise, I hadn't taken a proper breath and I plunged deep, my lungs starting to hurt right away — Where was the surface? I waggled my arms in a circle, bringing around my trunk and legs, oh, my chest hurt, not enough air in it. There's the light; stroke for the surface; make it; hold on; kick — I broke the surface and gasped in huge lungfuls, treading water, where were the others, the dinghies...? Margaret surfaced with a rush off to my right. She gulped for air and I yelled, "Chris??"

"Dad!" I heard behind me.

Without turning, I said, "Let's go!", because I now saw the dinghies in front of us. I started to breast stroke — the stroke that I did most easily, the stroke I could keep up the longest. The boats were near us, overturned, fortunately, so they dragged. Margaret, doing a crawl, got there slightly ahead of me. When I reached her, we pulled down on the Avon's lifeline together and the dinghies righted. Backing up, we grabbed onto the lifeline again, then the gunwale and

I said, "Ready? Go." We hauled ourselves up, onto, and into the boat.

Turning, I saw Chris just reaching for the lifeline. "Come on, son," I said.

"Wait," he said. He hung there for a long moment as we fell and rose with the giant swells. He looked up. "Dad, will you baptize me?" he asked.

I was taken aback. Chris had expressed interest in being baptized when younger, but we'd discouraged him. We'd said that it was a big step and that he'd do better to wait, become a little more mature, get more understanding. Recently, before the wreck, he'd mentioned it again. Now, apparently he'd been giving it serious thought.

I said, "You really understand what this is? Is this what you want?"

"Yeah, it's what I want," he said.

I looked into his eyes and saw a kind of hopeful serenity there. "All right," I said. "I'll take you by the hair. You'll have to let go, totally trust yourself to my hand. Let yourself immerse. I'll bring you back up. Do you understand?"

"Yes," he said. I took hold of his hair.

"Let go." He sank beneath the surface. I pulled him back up, and he grabbed the lifeline.

"I baptize you," I said, "in the name of the Father, the Son, and the Holy Spirit."

8:00 a.m.
Day nineteen
November 28, 1982
Colin Busch home
Kawa Kawa, Bay of Islands
New Zealand

The phone rang and Colin heard a voice on the other end saying, "Mr. Colin Busch? This is the Bay of Islands police, my name is Inspector Chaney. I'd like to talk to you about a missing sea vessel, the *Vamonos*."

"Good. Go ahead, Inspector."

"We've been contacted by the Honolulu Coast Guard, which in turn was responding to their California counterparts at the urging of a Mr. Leonard Smith, who I believe is a relative of the family on that vessel." Colin smiled wryly to himself. "We understand there is some urgency about this matter, sir, so if you could help us get the procedure underway, we can proceed."

"Anything I can do."

"Right then. What we'll need is a statement from you of the facts of the case and from anyone else who can give us an idea of what we're dealing with. From that, I hope, we'll have enough to initiate our harbor search."

"You'll have the statement as soon as we can draft it, Inspector, but a harbor search is not going to turn up anything. These people would never have made port and failed to apprise us that they were safe. They would have known we would be biting our nails with anxiety all the while they were out of radio contact. They would have immediately phoned us — the very first thing — and said, 'Sorry about the worries.

We're okay. We're safe.' They're not in any harbor."

"I take your point, Mr. Busch. I'll bear that in mind. We do have to do the harbor search. It's procedure. But... all right then, I won't wait for its completion before I bring in Search and Rescue. You get me that statement, telex it through your local police — I'll give you our telex number, and I'll rush this through."

After hanging up, Colin walked into the breakfast room where all his guests were sitting, helping themselves to eggs and kidney pie. "The police need a statement from us about Bob and Margaret. I think if you all help me with what you know, we can get some action here finally."

Nancy said, "Do you have a typewriter? I can type."

For nearly an hour, the yachties and the land base operator dictated a statement covering the history of the sailing sloop, structural problems, engine problems, speculation that the crew may have been bringing it to New Zealand for repairs, what the emergency equipment consisted of, and that there had been stored on the deck, since Papeete, water canisters for use in quick evacuation. Also given was a narrative of the check-ins with the Pacific Maritime Net and with 'the cockroach net.' Included were the position reports from November seventh through November ninth, and the course change. Also a description of the noted positions of Beveridge and Haran Reefs, and the ambiguity attached to these. Added was a detailed visual description of the vessel and attached was a copy of a photograph. Everything that was a fact was stated emphatically as one. Everything that was speculation was clearly stated to be so. They all signed it.

"Right," said Colin. "Let's get this on the wire."

———————

In the afternoon, I gouged out my biggest boils. New ones were coming in but I was obsessed with the older, larger ones. They'd grown to the size of golf balls. The two on my right elbow I'd watched grow into each other, closer and closer every day. Now they'd met under my skin.

I gouged them daily. Would have been nice if we'd managed to hold on to the alcohol towelettes we'd had the first days in the dinghies. Could have wiped the things when I finished.

Margaret, sitting at her usual place in the stern, had gouged some of hers earlier. Chris sat next to me, steering. I handed the sail needle to Margaret, saying, "I rinsed it off."

A booby bird landed on the gunwale.

It stood perched directly behind an unaware Margaret, calmly and stupidly looking at nothing in particular. It was about two feet high, with white feathers and a four inch bill.

Chris muttered low, "There's a bird right behind you." Her eyes opened wide. It had coasted in, without a flap of its wings.

"How tall is it?" she whispered.

"Like this," I said, spreading my hands slowly.

"Grab it, Margaret," said Chris.

She slowly raised her right arm to chest height, then swung around in a flash and got one of its legs. It immediately flapped its wings furiously, rising up, but its webbed foot prevented it from slipping out of her grasp. It ducked its head and pecked her hand viciously, but she held on. Chris and I got to her about the same time.

"Take it, take it!" she yelled, turning the bird toward us. I grabbed its other leg and she let go of hers. The thing was flapping and wriggling like mad, trying to get away. I squeezed as hard as I could. It wouldn't get away.

It pecked my hand pretty good, took some little chunks of flesh. I did my best to slap its beak away as it stabbed at me again and again. Chris swung his arm over its wings and pressed them to the bird's sides. Then he wrapped his other arm around it.

"Hold it, Chris, I'll get the paddle," I yelled. "Ready?" I let go and got the oar from behind me. "Watch your head," I said, and he leaned back. I whacked the bird on the side of the skull and its head swung sideways and right back up. I hit it on the forehead, and it went down and up. It struggled fiercely in Chris's arms and I brought the oar down again, this time connecting with its beak. It quieted for a moment, and I hit it again on the back of its skull. I hit it again.

"Is it dead?" breathed Margaret.

Chris, still with his arms around it, said, "No. It must just be stunned. It's breathing."

Margaret handed me the ever-useful needle, I held the bird's head below the beak, cut into the flesh and ripped. The feathered flesh parted and blood spurted. Holding it over the side now, I got the needle under another piece and ripped. Blood continued to flow and I hoped it would die without waking up. I got under another piece of neck and ripped it, then another. The body shivered slightly and died.

I continued around the neck, ripping small pieces until I had separated the skin all around. I sliced through the flesh until the head was mostly severed, then cracked the neck bone in two. I cut the rest and threw the head over the side.

I looked at the blood seeping from the neck knowing full well that as Christians we would never drink blood as others might. We drained the blood into the ocean and Chris and I prepared for what looked like a long, tedious job, plucking it and then skinning it with the sail needle. We began at the neck, pulling feathers for about a minute. Then, surprisingly, as we pinched the feathered flesh at the base of the neck and pulled, the skin started to come away from the muscle with the feathers, which then would release from it.

"Grab a handful near the top," I told Chris. I did so as well. "Pull downward." The skin came away from the muscle and we peeled it down, like taking off a coat.

I opened the bird up, bit by bit, with the needle, being careful not to break the bladder or bowels. When I was a kid, we'd lived just down from where Dodger Stadium is now, and there'd been plenty of space out there for livestock before they built the freeway. We'd had rabbits and chickens and my dad had taught me how to strip and gut them for the dinner table. That had been a long time before. Since then, I had once killed a pigeon needlessly, with a BB gun. I'd felt so bad as soon as I'd done it that I'd given the rifle away.

I took out the booby bird's intestines and all the inedible parts.

"Let's save some for bait," said Margaret. Always practical. The rest I threw over the side. After thanking God for this unexpected bounty, I reached back into the warm interior, got out the liver and heart.

"Liver, madam?" I asked.

"Yes, please, and a cold white wine, perhaps."

"I'll send the sommelier and he can show you the wine list."

"This is delicious," she said. "And *warm*." It was the first warm food she'd had for more than two miserable, chilled weeks.

"May I have some breast?" Chris asked politely.

"Certainly, young sir," I said. "I'll be carving in a moment."

I bit into the heart, and the feeling of warmth was terrific. Then the moistness of the thing! I closed my eyes and felt pleasure course through my starved, weak body. The heart was moist and meaty and delicious. "It's warm, Chris."

"Oh wow, right. Do you want me to cut the breast?"

"No, I'll do it for you." I painstakingly ripped off a piece with the needle, then handed it to him. He bit into it, and his eyes closed, too. "But no wine for you, young sir," I said.

With his eyes still closed, he smiled. "This is just fine."

"It really is good, isn't it? Bob, would you cut me a piece of that?"

Happily, we sat and slowly ate the bird. The flesh was a bit stringier than the heart but I didn't care at all about that. It was wonderful. It was the good life. Even though the sommelier never did show up.

We ate about three-quarters of the bird and decided we'd stop to save some for the following day. It was more than we'd eaten in nineteen days. We were almost satisfied.

We hung the rest of the carcass from the mast.

"Oh! Dad, look out for my leg!"

"I'm just trying to turn on my side — just steer the boat."

"Bob! Oww! Don't do that!"

"Where'm I supposed to put my foot?!"

"Well not — Ow! Stop it!"

"Just a minute."

"Your foot is behind my knee! You know I'm really sore there —"

"All right! There, is that better? Is everybody happy??"

Day twenty
November 29, 1982
Daybreak

We're floating so gently. Yes, ah yes, there's a group of islands here, small and beautiful. Nice, it's a lagoon. I can smell bananas, yes, there on the trees, bunches of them, green ones. No yellow ones? Oh sure, there are lots of yellow ones, ripe. I'm hungry. Coconuts there. Drink from those, eat the pudding. Almost there. Natives! They see us! Yes, we're the Americans! They've heard about us. They're happy to be the ones who found us. Lots of fat ones, smiling, they look so clean and fresh. Cheering, gesturing... Oh! Sure! The water's shallow here. Two or three feet. No need to wait for them to get us. Just step out, walk over. They're so happy to see us. It's finally over. Gotta just get myself up. Good. Better get on my knees, step over—

"Dad!"

"Bob! What are you doing??"

They're grabbing me. They don't see. "We can walk out."

"No we can't, Dad! That's the ocean!"

"No, no. It's shallow here. We can walk. Let me go, Chris!"

"Bob! Stop! You can't get —"

"See the people? The natives? They're right there."

They were holding me down. I'm not very strong, anymore. What are they doing? Pushing me down. My butt hurts. He's hurting my arm, too. "Chris. You're hurting me."

"Don't get out of the boat, Dad."

"All right, all right. Why don't you want to go?" I looked at the island and it was the sea. Where were the people? "Where are the people, Chris?"

"There aren't any people, Bob." My wife was still holding me down, too. "You had a dream."

"You don't have to hold me, Margaret. What about the bananas?"

"It was a dream, Bob."

There were no bananas and no coconuts. We were at sea.

Chris brought down the bird carcass. It had completely dried out, flapping there in the wind, and we were able to pull the meat off in strips. It was chewy. It was bird jerky. I didn't like it much, and neither did Margaret. Chris said it was better than the day before. The thing was dry, very dry. We ate it all, Chris even chewing on the delicate bones. It gave you a big thirst. We passed around the can filled with water. Five-and-a-bit ounces each. This was the second to last can. The last one would go that afternoon.

I lay back in the dinghy and tried to rest. I wasn't sleeping more than twenty minutes or a half hour at a time, I think. I'd find a position which seemed comfortable, say to myself: There, that's better, that's comfortable; then ten minutes later it'd be impossibly painful, so I'd try to find another position, finally saying to myself: There, that's comfortable...

"Why don't You answer our prayers??" I shouted. The sky remained impassive. "Don't You see how weak we are?! We've been out here all these days. We've prayed a hundred times, hundreds of times to be rescued — Why don't You do something for us?"

"Bob, come on. You know that Jehovah doesn't owe us anything we're asking for."

"But we're in a terrible, terrible state."

"We got ourselves into it. Human error. And the bad weather."

That made some sense. In fact, I knew it was true. Knew it logically — could remember myself saying that very type of thing in the past. But this was, this was too much...

"Every day," she said, "there's the hope that today He'll answer our prayers, send someone to find us."

That was true, she was right.

"Jehovah doesn't owe us a rescue," she repeated. "He's not responsible for our predicament."

True.

We are going to die out here. No doubt about it. I'm so thirsty. Need water. This is a bad way to die, suffering to death. It could be an easier way. Thirsty. Have some water.

I picked up the five gallon jug and twisted the top off. Lifting it, I drank the warm, clean water.

"Bob! What are you *doing*! Chris grab him!"

He reached over and yanked the jug from my lips. She had her hands on it too. They easily got it away from me.

"How much is left, Margaret?"

"About half a pint. He drank half what was there. Oh, Bob..."

The water was good. Didn't feel so thirsty now.

11:00 a.m.
Colin Busch office
Kawa Kawa Post Office
Bay of Islands
New Zealand

"Look. I've been calling since nine o'clock. I want to speak to someone if Mr. Miller still isn't in... All right, I'll take Captain Hillary." If I must, he thought.

"I was planning on calling you, Mr. Busch. You'll be happy to know that we've instituted a harbor search."

God give me patience, thought Colin. "Captain, I know the police instituted a harbor search. They told me yesterday they would straight away. I told them, as I've already told you, that a harbor search would show up nothing, and I told them why. We need you to do something here."

"Also, you know, there's a good chance these people simply had a change of plan. Put in somewhere else, maybe Tonga or Fiji."

"Same thing, there: They'd never do that without telling us at their first opportunity."

"Maybe they haven't had an opportunity yet."

"Where do you think they set out for? Canada?"

"Look here, Mr. Busch. It's my responsibility to assess the situation and what happens here happens on my say-so, which is also my responsibility."

"All right, all right. Did you get a copy of our statement?"

"Yes, I have it here, and that's what I was going to call you about. I have a few problems with it. First you say, 'They were coming directly to New Zealand from Rarotonga.' But then you say they were west-northwest of

Rarotonga. You don't sail that way if you're coming to New Zealand."

"No. Of course not. We felt they made an error in navigation."

"Are you an experienced sailor, Mr. Busch?"

"Me? No, I'm a landlubber. I can plot positions and courses, though."

"There are some things you wouldn't understand without a familiarity with the sea."

"I'll do this then: I'll get Dave Ingalls, who also signed that statement, on the line with us. He's a sailor. Will you hold the line?"

"Oh, all right."

Colin called home and reached Dave. "Dave, this is this Captain Hillary I told you about. He gets me crazy, but we have to get past him. If I start to threaten to beat him silly, stop me. I don't know what his maritime qualifications are, but he's arguing about the radioed positions, so I thought you ought to handle this." Colin completed the three-way connection. He had Hillary repeat his objection.

Dave listened to it, then said, "Well, when you first leave harbor you guess your way, you dead reckon your way roughly for a couple of days until you settle down and you can take a sun shot. Sometimes you find out you're not quite where you thought you were so you adjust your course. It was cloudy out there on those first few days. They told us on the radio that they hadn't been able to get even one sighting, that they hoped to get one that noon, and they did. It threw us at first, too, their position turning out so far north — that is, when we discussed it later — but then we figured something like that must have happened. They dead-reckoned. It was faulty for some reason. They corrected."

Colin said, "There's also the possibility that Bob was a little worried about the boat taking on water and decided to keep a more northerly course, closer to Tonga, so in case he had a problem he could put in there."

"But he headed not just west, Mr. Busch, but north of west."

"Maybe," Dave said, "something threw his dead reckoning off. If you put some beer cans over the side to cool, or something like that, and they're near the compass, that can put you wrong by a few degrees until you take a shot and find that something's amiss."

"Yes, well, this is all speculation, really. But if it's so, then that contradicts your statement. Because there you say that they were coming directly to New Zealand from Rarotonga."

"...That's right," Colin said, questioningly.

"But the direct route from Rarotonga to New Zealand is southwest."

"Yes. Right."

"But here their position clearly shows they were heading west-northwest. They weren't heading directly to New Zealand from Rarotonga because the direct route is southwest."

"Bloody hell! They were coming directly here because they weren't going anywhere else in between!"

"But that's not what direct means, Mr. Busch."

"Do you mean that I didn't use the right word?! Are you saying I should have used — 'non-stop'?? Is that it??"

"Uhh, Colin. I think that's right," said Dave. "The captain's right. We should have said 'non-stop'. Much better word. More accurate."

"Yes, indeed," said Hillary.

"Okay, good," said Colin. "Tell me, Captain. Are you going to do anything about finding our friends out there?"

"Just as soon as I see the results of the harbor search, I'm going to start making some decisions..."

The swells are up again. Very high. Every afternoon, they get high. Much too high. Put this piece of rag over my face. Darker. Better.

"Dad, take the oar, will you?"

I didn't answer him. The dinghy rose under me. Too high. Not right for a human being.

"Dad, you need to take the oar."

I need, huh? I need to lay here.

"What is it, Bob? Bob...?"

She tried to take the rag off my face, but I snatched it. I held my hand on top of it.

"He's... so weak, Chris."

Yeah, I'm weak. I'm tired.

"All right. I'll keep the tiller for a while more, then you take it, Margaret."

"Okay."

Yeah. Let him make the decisions for a while. See how he likes it. See how he deals with the sea having him to play with.

Day twenty-one
November 30, 1982

Without food or drink, death usually occurs within
about ten days (survival times are shorter in hot or cold
conditions and at high levels of activity).

— American Medical Association Encyclopedia of Medicine

No food, no water.

Chris said, "Maybe we can drink a little sea water. I've swallowed it accidentally, plenty of times. You know, while swimming. What do you think, Dad?"

I thought I was awfully thirsty. But try to be logical. It'd probably dehydrate us. Yes, it'd definitely dehydrate us. But was it better than nothing?

"Drinking salt water will dehydrate us," I said.

"Maybe we could limit it to, say, one gulp a day," said Chris.

"What do you think, Bob? He's got a point about swallowing some when you're swimming."

"Yes. Yes, all right. One gulp a day."

"I'm gonna take mine, now," Chris said and turned to his hands and knees, leaned over the side. He immersed his head briefly and brought it up, streaming and grinning.

"Yum."

Margaret, sitting, leaned over and did the same.

I bent over the side and took my gulp of ocean. It was repulsive. Not the taste — that was, well, salt water. It was the fact of letting the sea into my body. I tried to think that I was using it against itself, but that didn't work. I was drinking the enemy. And the enemy was probably laughing at me for it.

Margaret said, "But just the one gulp." Chris grinned at her. "You were thinking the same thing as me, weren't you?" she laughed.

"Yeah. I was thinking, 'That was good. How 'bout another?'"

"Right," she smiled, "but we can't."

"No."

I wasn't smiling.

"How you doin', Dad?"

"That dream yesterday was so real. I saw those villagers and that lagoon. They were so happy to see us. I think that was the strongest part of it — someone showing us some kindness."

"We have each other," Margaret said.

"I know."

"We're together," said Chris.

I got the needle to scrape my boils.

9:00 a.m.
Colin Busch office
Kawa Kawa Post Office
Bay of Islands
New Zealand

"Mr. Miller is still out sick, Mr. Busch. You were talking with Captain Hillary yesterday, weren't you? Would you like to be put through to him again?"

"Yes."

"Hillary."

"Colin Busch, Captain. How are you?"

"Fine, Mr. Busch. And you?"

"Fine. So I'm calling to see if there's been any progress."

"Yes, well, the police have just about completed their harbor search. They've not turned anything up."

"All right."

"Now this idea that your friends got into trouble on the... let's see, ninth of November. What's your basis for that?"

"Well, that's the last we heard from them. It's logical to suppose that they got into trouble in the next few hours. They were to check in again at ten the following morning with their friend's network, and they didn't. So sometime late on the ninth or early the following morning."

"Now, 'suppose' is the very word you use, 'logical to suppose,' so really that's all we're dealing with here, isn't it?"

Colin, with his free hand, clenched the edge of his desk. "...Yes, that is the logical supposition."

"But I can't muster the nation's armed forces just on your supposition, of course. I'm sure you can see that."

Colin didn't reply.

"And," Hillary continued, "it's only supposition on your part that they were coming directly to New Zealand, because they weren't."

"Only an idiot, a bloody idiot would insist that you must go straight across the sea to get where you're going! Ships don't sail straight — not even an aircraft flies dead straight!"

"Don't get shirty with me, Mr. Busch!"

"I'm —" More quietly, he said, "Bloody hell. I'm not going round and round with you on this stupid subject of coming direct again. Now look. What we're concerned about here, what this whole line of reasoning stems from, is that if you look at the course they were running at the time, Beveridge Reef and Haran Reef were very possibly on the line of their course correction."

"Yes, and I've looked at that, but really, I don't think they could have hit such a small outcrop as these are."

Colin squeezed his eyes shut and took the receiving end of the phone between his teeth. Then, into the receiver, he said evenly, "It's not impossible to hit anything. If it's physically there you can hit it."

"It's so unlikely."

"...Look. Why don't you talk to one of the boat-owners? Dave again, or Harry. They're the experts. You seamen should be talking directly."

"... Well... all right. Have them call me."

"I'll have them call you."

Dusk wasn't far off. The afternoon swells hadn't been as terrible as usual. There was more chop than we were used to seeing, less swell. We rattled around a little more from it, but at least the sea wasn't —

"Land!! I see land," shouted Margaret.

I twisted around and looked forward. I couldn't see anything.

"Where??" yelled Chris.

"Dead ahead!!"

I still couldn't see anything. Chris asked, "You mean that little haze?"

"Yeah," she said. "It's hazy and small. Dead ahead." I knew Margaret had very good long vision. Could she be right?

"I think you're right," said Chris. He got on his knees and stretched. "It's land!"

I saw something. Surrounded in haze and seeming too small to be an island. Margaret cried, "I bet we're seeing the top of a volcano!"

And she was right. In the next twenty minutes, the failing light revealed a conical shape that kept widening as we approached. It was still probably far away — we were only seeing the very top, but we were heading straight for it. We threw our arms around each other and kissed and cried. We thanked Jehovah for putting us in the path of this island, this safety, this end to our suffering when we needed it most. We talked of fruit on the island, and fresh water, and maybe natives. We discussed the best way to find a village, how far we'd probably have to walk; weak as we were, we'd find a way. Whatever we had to do, we would, because now we were saved.

At least that's what we thought, then.

FIFTEEN

Day twenty-two
December 1, 1982
Dawn

We'd probably come ten miles through the night sea, and daybreak showed the island quite clearly, still perhaps twenty miles away. It indeed had a volcano on it amid mountainous, rocky terrain. We weren't close enough to distinguish any trees. In fact we couldn't see the lower portions at all, we were still too distant. There were other islands around it as well.

By noon, we could see how big they were. We were probably fourteen or fifteen miles away, still. We began to hear a low roar. We wondered what it was.

In the following half-hour, the roar steadily increased. What on earth was it? We began to see peculiar white water on the horizon. As we moved up, the white water started to take shape as a spray. It revealed itself, quickly intermittent, higher and higher until it reached twenty feet.

"There's a reef between us and the island," I said. We'd all been peering at this phenomenon in our path, and when we realized what it was, we knew we were in trouble.

"We've got to get ready for it," Chris said.

A reef in the ocean, even one below the surface, is land to the oncoming waves. They go up high as they approach, with greatly increased speed, and crash down onto the obstruction. And it was going to be taking us with it.

"I think we'd better separate the dinghies," I said.

"Oh, Bob, no! We're supposed to stay together!"

"Margaret," I said, "we'll still be together. We can even keep them tied with the fifteen-foot line. But this set-up is too awkward. It'll be like when you body-surf to shore. You know how it throws you around."

I saw them both looking at me, thinking over what I'd said. They were probably wondering how rational I was.

Something in the prospect of going over the reef, like an incredible roller-coaster with the seas so high, excited me, cheered me. And made me more myself.

"With this set-up, the forward dinghy will be in a different part of the breaking wave from the aft one. It'll be chaos. We'd have a better chance riding the surf in complete, separate boats.

"I'm scared," she said.

"You and I can go in the Avon and Chris in the hard dinghy."

"Chris, what do you think?"

"I think he's right, Margaret. Sounds right."

"Okay."

So we unlashed the dinghies. Chris stepped forward into the Sandpiper and finished undoing the line that had connected them. As the Avon came away, it started taking the seas more roughly without the stabilizing effect of the Sandpiper's length. Also with the exposed stern of it now being our leading edge. I considered turning it around using the oar, but then the windsurfer line would be under us, or would have to be reconnected behind us. If I didn't turn it, though, we wouldn't have the bow of the dinghy forward to help us stay straight. I decided to turn it and reconnect the surfer; we'd need every advantage we could get.

I retied the fifteen foot line, which Chris was still holding, to the gunwale, and he did the same in the hard dinghy. As he paid it out to its limit, out to our left, he looked closely at each section of the line. Most of these nylon lines were pretty rotten by now. I thought this the best one we had. He said, "This'll probably hold okay. It's not too bad. I'm gonna take down the sail and lash it."

We had two remaining life jackets. They were there with Margaret and me. I should have thought about them sooner. I called to Chris, "Take one of the jackets. Margaret and I will be together. If we have to, we can hold each other, make one do for both of us." He thought about it for a moment, then agreed and hauled on the line, bringing us closer. Margaret waited until the boats almost touched before tossing the jacket to him: the seas were swelling at about thirty feet, trough to crest; take no chances.

I tied the oar to the gunwale. I got the thwart, the inflated oblong cushion that comes with the dinghy as a seat, and straddled it. I was in the bow, facing the reef. Margaret knelt in her usual space behind me. "Put on the jacket, honey," I said.

"Bob, you take it."

"No."

"Bob, I'm so frightened for you. You're so — fragile, now. You move so weakly — Please take the jacket."

"No. I'm all right." I kept looking forward. I heard her sigh and pull the jacket to her.

I was all right. Ahead I could see the wave spray leaping

up ten or fifteen feet in the air. We were moving faster and faster, and the swells were reaching twenty feet. It was exhilarating! Roller-coasters scare the wits out of me, but I always go on them anyway. This was like that. It seemed that way to me.

"The dinghies won't sink," I called over my shoulder. "You know that."

"I know this one can't sink as long as the reef doesn't rip open the gun'ls. And I know that you can't sink the Sandpiper by just filling it with water. But the fiberglass could crack."

"The fiberglass won't crack."

"I'm just scared, Bob," she said.

"We'll be all right, honey. So will Chris." We were heading up to a crest and I could see that we were only two hundred feet away now. "Okay, hang onto the outside lifelines! Whatever happens, hang onto the boat. If we go under, it'll bring us back up with it." I grabbed the forward part of the lines and held tight.

The roar was getting incredible. As we'd approach a crest, I could see the shooting spray reveal itself more and more. Then, at the top, you could see the reef it was breaking on — we were that close. I got a charge of excitement, of adrenaline. I felt strong. A flush of strength to get me through.

Down into a trough, Chris out fifteen feet to our left, the roar muffled; then up again, louder and louder, at the top looking down — like looking down from the largest roller-coaster I'd ever seen. Close now, maybe the next crest will do it. Down into the trough, the roar all around, big sections of agitated bubbles, white water, chop, roar —

"Oh!!" cried Margaret.

"It's okay, honey!" I shouted. "Just hold on, whatever

you do! Stay with the boat!"

"Oh, Bob!!"

"When we get there, grab a deep breath and hold on!!"

We crested. This is it. There's the reef, shallow water coursing over it as the trough moved through down there.

Our crest started breaking, its top curling forward. It lifted us and roiled around us as we were pushed forward by its incredible surge breaking at our backs. Down, down, what a ride, my eyes stared open as we dropped. Here it comes. Here it comes. We reached the water surface and instantly from behind the wave crashed on top of us, forcing us under. A falling mountain of water, booming around us, forcing the dinghy down, everywhere water churning and roiling, a giant hand mashing us under it. The cushion between my legs trembled, trying to escape — I clenched it with my legs, bent forward there underwater. The dinghy shuddered violently to be under, its buoyancy jerking us to a halt. It propelled us back up and, as my head broke the surface, the cushion between my legs leaped free and rocketed past my face, shooting into the air.

The Avon floated quickly forward on the reef, full of water and riding low. I gasped for air and could hear Margaret doing the same. I shot a glance over the side and saw a table reef, like Beveridge, and we were sweeping along it.

Where was Chris? I looked left and saw the snapped line and farther on the capsized Sandpiper. Then I saw him in the water, struggling to swim to the boat. The reef must be lower, deeper there, I thought.

We were moving forward and to our right as the current coursed across the reef — it wasn't sitting square to the seas. Margaret shouted, "Chris!!" and jumped over the port gunwale. Kneeling in the two or three feet of water here, she hauled on the lifeline to halt the dinghy's progress. It dragged her with it, she skidding on her knees but holding on. My weight was defeating her.

Chris, about twenty-five feet away from us now, yelled, "Dad! Get out of the boat!!"

"The coral will cut my feet!"

"Just do it! Get out! Now!"

I was shocked for a second. Did he know better than I did? Wait, of course he did — I was losing it: that dream I believed, the drinking water I took.

I flopped over the port gunwale, my arms still inside, clutching the dinghy. It stopped.

Chris righted the Sandpiper and quickly hand-paddled nearer to us, then jumped out and let the dinghy float to us, holding it back with the snapped line. Another wave broke and water surged at us. We held on.

Chris came up. "Oh, man! I'm glad you listened to me — I thought I was gonna lose ya."

"Yeah. That was good that you — whoa! Watch out — wave!" It thundered around and past us.

"Hey, we did it," shouted Margaret over the roar, her voice full of relief. "We did it!" We looked at each other for a moment. Then she looked around. "We didn't lose the windsurfer! There it is!" And there too was the sock, wrapping itself around it to and fro.

Another wave crashed around us. "Did you see that cushion fly up, Margaret?!"

"Yeah! Wow!"

Chris said, "We better get into these dinghies. Wave coming." He jerked the painter of the Sandpiper, quickly tied it to our Avon, then held onto his dinghy. When the breaker had rushed through and past, Margaret and I crawled into the soft dinghy.

Chris hopped into the Sandpiper, said, "Grab onto my gun'l," and Margaret in the Avon stern, did. He quickly lashed the sterns back-to-back again, the next breaker moving us along. He threw another piece of line over it and pulled it taut.

I looked in the direction we were going and said, "We're almost at the edge."

"Is there a lagoon, do you think?" Chris called.

"Should be," said Margaret, hopefully.

The next breakers carried us farther across the reef, closer and closer to the edge. Then we spilled into the ocean.

The big reefs surround clutches of islands, sitting in big lagoons. That's the kind of reef we hoped we were on. In the distance we could see the big island dead ahead and the smaller ones off to both sides. To the left was a motu. They're small islands, usually around a hundred feet by a hundred feet, too small to support a community. This one had vegetation though, thick and green, doubtless growing coconuts and who knew what else. And there'd be fresh water. Had to be to support vegetation. We were quickly into swells, but that could be wash-through from the ocean's action outside the reef. The seas should calm into a lagoon beyond the breakwater a vast reef provides. These didn't. These seas continued to rise.

It'd been a little table reef, like the one where we'd come to harm. Now we were not in a lagoon. Now we could not easily row the dinghies to the motu off to port. Now we were going to be carried where the sea wanted.

But fortunately, we thought, it was carrying us to that big volcano island.

Noon
Sailing Schooner **Deliverance**
Under sail off French Polynesia

Immediately after being switched on, the radio picked up a voice calling the boat's call sign: "Lima Romeo *** Echo Echo Alpha, this is Zebra Lima *** Bravo Kilo Delta from Bay of Islands, New Zealand. Standing by..."

The captain, who was also the licensed radio operator, responded with his call sign and, "This is Dave Higgins on *Deliverance*. What can I do for you, Bay of Islands?"

"I'm glad to reach you, Dave. You don't know me, but I was talking with Mac in Hawaii — Larry McPherson — and he said you were just the man to help us, if you would. He said that with all your nautical experience and your influence as an attorney — well, let me explain. We have a situation here..." He went on to describe their fears for the crew of the *Vamonos* and the administrative foot-dragging he'd been encountering in New Zealand. Dave asked questions throughout.

"Now, give me their position reports, including the weather," he said.

That finished, Colin asked, "So what do you think?"

"I think the first thing I'm going to do when I get off with you is make a radio telephone call to Search and Rescue Wellington. They're the ones who were concerned; they're the one's who were contacted by the American authorities. I'll get them to call Auckland. They can't insist that Auckland get going, but if I light enough of a fire under them, some of it may carry over."

"Then I'll sit down and calculate the arcs of drift from the two reefs. No one's done that. It's a bit involved, so it'll take me some time. The thing is, if we can get a visual picture of what would have happened if they did come to grief there, it would limit the search area. That'd make it a simpler, less expensive operation, with more chance of quick success. Should make it more attractive to the powers-that-be."

"That sounds quite good, Dave. I appreciate all this."

"Don't give it another thought, Colin. If Bob, Margaret and Chris are out there — Don't give it another thought."

Late afternoon and the big island was only a few miles away. Now we could, as we'd hoped, see tree tops over the horizon, so we were maybe five or six miles out. We were talking again about fruit and water and natives when Margaret said, "Are we turning?" She sat, as usual, facing forward, and didn't take her eyes off the island. "Chris, are you steering us to starboard, somehow?"

"No. I'm not doing anything different. Anyhow, we always steer as far starboard as we can."

"We're definitely veering to the right."

I'd twisted around as soon as she'd asked her first question. She was right. So what was going on?

We talked it over, more and more urgently. Chris steered to port as much as he could. It made little difference. If any.

"Wait a minute," Chris said. "I see what it is. Of course the current's not going to flow straight at the island. The land is in the way, so the sea just goes around it."

We let this horrible thought sink in.

"What are we gonna do?" Margaret asked him.

"Chris," I said, "take the windsurfer and the paddle and make for shore. Get some help."

Chris hesitated but Margaret didn't.

"No! No way can he get to that island. Don't you know how weak he is? He'd drown."

"I probably would," he said, after a moment. "And that'd even leave you without the paddle. And we don't know that there's anybody on that island, anyway."

They were right. I don't know how I could think that was the right thing to do. But the frustration! So close to this island and no way to get to it!

And didn't that mean that any big island we approached we'd be taken around? Were we going to keep being shown islands, their safety, their food and water, and then, like Tantalus, see them recede, drop away out of reach?

I heard Margaret crying. I looked at her. There were no tears coming out of her eyes. Her body didn't have the water for it.

———————

Colin Busch office
Kawa Kawa Post Office
Bay of Islands
New Zealand

"Colin, phone."

Going to his desk, Colin picked up the receiver.

"Mr. Busch? Miller, Coordinator Search and Rescue, Auckland."

"Ah yes, Mr. Miller."

"I've been talking to our Search and Rescue people in Wellington. And, you see, they have their maritime advisors over there, just as I have mine here. Well, I've just finished a long conversation with them."

"Yes?"

"Tomorrow morning we're sending up a plane."

SIXTEEN

Day twenty-three
December 2, 1982

It's the hour before dawn and Chris and I are leaving Michel's hut. We're working our way through the shrubbery with the Polynesian in the lead, down to where his skiff is. "Do you start this early every morning?" I ask him, but he just smiles over his shoulder at us. He doesn't say much. His English isn't good. Maybe he speaks more when he's with other Polynesians. We're putting the big axes for cutting the coconuts into the skiff and motoring out into the lagoon. The early breeze feels fine. I'm hungry, though. We'll eat lunch later. Great.

Outside another hut Chris looks at the huge stack of coconuts and he whistles. Michel rolls a few down to a clear spot and splits them, one after the other. The coconut water splashes up and onto me and I want to drink it. I look down, and it's soaking into my bright red flower shirt. With his ax, Michel scoots the coconut halves across the ground. There's a little pile there already. The natives'll get money for them as copra. He rolls a few more down. I pick up an

ax and stand next to him. I split a coconut and Michel
smiles at me with his white, white teeth. Chris goes around
to the other side of the pile with the other ax.

Time to eat. Time to eat. I wonder what Michel has to
cook. He picks up a burlap sack and walks down to the
sand. He kneels and rustles through the weeds. I know
there are crabs there. He plucks a shell from the sand. The
crab is sticking out of it slightly. Michel twists it out of the
shell, it's easy to get at it because it protrudes. Well, that's
because it's not really his shell. He's a hermit crab. He left
his own shell, his first home, and went out to find a new
one. He found a shell, too, but it wasn't good enough for
him after a while. He set out again across the sand, across
the big swells, so big he was amazed, and then he was
frightened, and he got into this shell but it was too small for
him, too cramped, but he was afraid of the sea, afraid, he
was so exposed, and Michel's hand comes down toward *me,*
the huge thumb and forefinger held close together, near,
nearer, they pinch the sides of my head and start to pull me
from the shell. The fingertips hurt my skull and my neck
stretches, my body stuck, the boils hurting down my
shoulders, oh the elbows hurt so much, he's pulling me out,
hips and legs screaming with pain and then I'm out in the
burning sunlight, so hot on my naked, soft body. He opens
the sack and throws me inside. I go scraping down the wall
of it, the burlap raking my body as I fall. I roll around the
bottom. I'm the only one there. It's so dark. I look up for
some light and see Chris skidding down the side, screaming
— like when he was a child. No! Here comes Margaret into
the bag. No!

"No!!" I croaked. "No!" My eyes opened. The sun was
up and beating on me.

"Dad. You had a bad dream."

Chris, bleary-eyed, holding the oar, looks back at the sea, keeping watch for rogues.

I stared at him for a good while.

9:00 a.m.
Orion aircraft
Captain Johnston commanding
Altitude 1,000 feet

"There're the Kermadecs, sir. L'Esperance Rock dead ahead."

"I'm going down farther, gentlemen. From here on out, for the next twelve hours, I want all of you to have one eye down there and one eye on the sky around us. We're going to do this all as low as we can and I don't want any private planes or hot-air balloons suddenly on an intercept path. We're going to do this so low you'll be wiping surf from your brows."

Severe dehydration is likely to develop within a few days if no water is taken.... Symptoms and signs of water depletion include severe thirst, dry lips and tongue, an increase in heart rate and breathing, dizziness, confusion, and eventual coma.

— American Medical Association Encyclopedia of Medicine

The morning light revealed four new islands, all pretty large, all between three and ten miles ahead of us.

We were approaching the nearest island, off the port bow, and already the sea was taking us to starboard. I thought, "You think it's funny, don't you? You have all the answers, all the tricks." Then, "Why all this malice? All we did was sail on you. Is it an ancient hate? Have you hated men from the beginning of time, found them puny, ached to destroy them? Do you wait for your chance and when you get it, leap to it with relish? I'm very, very frightened of you. But I'll fight you. At least I have that left."

After we passed far enough, the sea took us back to port, resuming its former direction. I stared back at the island, back to land. Trees. That meant water. I saw a couple of little leaves floating on the low swell. Must have come from the island. One was close, so I plucked it out of the water and ate it. A little bitter. And faintly salty from the water. I saw Chris do the same with the leaf on his side. It was then that I noticed that the windsurfer was no longer following us......it was gone.

Orion aircraft
Captain Johnston commanding
10:30 a.m.

"Minerva reef to port, sir."

"All right. Changing course for it. Minerva's an outside possibility. But those drift-arcs that fella gave us are pretty convincing about Tonga. That's where I'd put my money if I had to."

"Eastern group, sir?"

"Maybe, Reg. Doesn't matter much what I'd bet, though. We'll proceed nice and orderly. We'll work the outer group, then the eastern group. Do it all."

"Hundreds of islands, there, sir."

"Yes. Now, Minerva first. Remember, no pre-conceptions — Look at everything, big, small, boat, raft, floating log. Everything."

"After Tonga, what then, Captain?"

"Then we work our way slowly east, heading for the elusive Beveridge Reef."

We'd passed the other three islands, now. It was mid-morning.

Chris said, "There's another one, a real small one, dead ahead."

I looked and saw, not an island, really, but a sandbar. It was about three miles ahead. I put my head over the side and took my gulp of sea water. My one per day. I lay back in the dinghy, totally exhausted. When would I die? Not today, probably. But maybe tomorrow.

Chris twisted back to see where we were heading. "You know, it's funny," he said. "We're not veering off."

Margaret looked up at the sandbar. "No? Well, that's probably because this thing's smaller, so the current doesn't have to shift so much to go around it."

"Yeah, that sounds right," he said.

The swells were beginning to pick up. A little early today. By noon, they were a pretty good size, almost ten feet. We were moving along at a fairly good clip. I wanted another gulp of water.

"We're still not veering off," said Margaret.

"No, we're not," said Chris.

"How far away are we?" I asked.

"Less than a mile, I think," said Chris.

I roused myself and twisted around. A mile seemed about right. The island was still dead ahead.

We watched it in silence. Slowly we approached it, still on line. I'd imagine we were veering, but after a minute I'd see that we weren't. We got closer and closer.

Margaret said, "How close do you think we'll get?"

"Don't know," said Chris. I could see that it was a barren little thing. It looked to have shale on the windward side, our side. We couldn't see the other. There were some darkish masses, very low down, that could have been shrubbery of some kind. The whole thing might be about sixty or seventy feet in radius from where it met the ocean to its high ground in the middle, "high" meaning about five feet above sea level. Not a tree on it.

Quarter of a mile. A thousand feet. Seven hundred. Four

hundred.

"We're still not veering!" said Chris, with tense excitement.

How close would the sea let us get? The sandbar was small, but it was solid ground, dry ground.

Two hundred feet. One fifty. A hundred. Fifty.

We began to veer to port.

"What are we gonna do??" Margaret shouted.

"Is that coral?!" yelled Chris.

I looked over the side. "Yes! Do you think you could reach it?!"

Chris scrambled up, grabbed a line and quickly knotted it to the lines lashing the dinghies. The coral heads we were seeing were two or three feet below the surface, some with rounded tops and branches below. He dove overboard ahead of the boat.

We were still veering to port and moving forward at the same time —- moving forward at a good pace with the swells about five feet now. Margaret and I could see Chris among the branches of coral, saw him down there being pulled along, the line yanking him back as he tried to kick for a coral head to his right. The dinghies, skewed slightly in his direction, moved beyond him continuing to port. Chris surfaced a second, drew a breath, dove again. We were coming up on another coral head, and he saw it, kicked ahead of the dinghies and reached it. He passed the line around it near the top, twice, held it. The line went taut, the dinghies lurched a little, the line held. He threw a sailor's knot in the line, then another. He looked up, kicked and broke the surface, gasping for breath.

"Fantastic," I shouted. "Just fantastic, Chris."

He grinned at me, grabbed the top of the Avon's gunwale,

and hauled himself upwards. Margaret grasped his arm and hoisted. When he clambered aboard, she threw her arms around him and began to cry, saying, "Chris, you did it!"

I tousled his wet hair and said, "You did great!"

"We're gonna reach land!" he yelled happily.

"When the winds die down, we'll paddle in," Chris had said. He'd also said, "No sweat," but I don't think any of us thought that was the case. Paddling against a current is never any fun and we had only one oar. We were all so weak.

The entire afternoon, we bobbed and stared at the sandbar. A dismal thing, a little glitch of land. It had no trees. The area of scrub brush, if that's what it was, seemed the only vegetation. We couldn't see the far side, of course, but the sandbar was only about five feet high at the center: There were no trees over there. We had to have water. And food. We were dying.

We had switched the anchor line to the bow of the Sandpiper. By four-thirty, the wind had died down and Chris judged that the sea was as calm as it was likely to get. We needed the remaining daylight to get there and, once ashore, to see what was there. The sail was already lowered and stowed. The mast, a pole really, I was going to use as an oar.

When we'd anchored to the coral head, the Avon had continued along and was now facing the sandbar. Chris said, "Okay, first let's do this: We'll see if we can make headway against the current. We can stay anchored for this, it's a test. Dad, can you make it into the Sandpiper?" I twisted around, got on my knees and crawled over the back-to-back sterns, over the seat and into the bow of the hard dinghy. I was closest to the coral head. I had the mast pole with me.

"Margaret," he said, "You and I'll be in the Avon. You'll have to paddle with your hands, okay? Okay. When I say go, we'll try to row straight back, try to slack the line, all right? Ready, Dad?"

"Ready."

"One, two, three, go!"

I dug in with the pole on the starboard side. It passed through the water too easily, but we started to move. Seven or eight strokes and I looked forward and down. "We're coming up on it, Chris. The coral head."

"Yeah, great, relax everybody." We coasted back away from the mooring and the line caught us at its limit.

"Okay, so we can move. So what we'll have to do is untie..."

"You know, Chris?" said Margaret, "I don't think we should just cast off, leaving the line. I'd really hate to lose anything else, just leave it behind."

I agreed with her. You never knew when you'd need something, something that seems useless, but later on makes all the difference.

"Okay," he said. "Well, you were probably making the least headway, Margaret, without a paddle or anything. I'm sure Dad and I could hold the boats in place by the coral head. Could you dive under and get us untied?"

"I could do that," she said.

I said, "You'd have to get back up here quick, honey."

"I know. I can do it."

"All right," Chris said. "So that's what we'll do. Once we're free, we'll try to head almost directly at the sandbar. The current will try to push us past. Well, it will push us that way. We'll try to go with it as little as we can, and mostly at the sandbar. If we can get close enough, we can get to the lee of it, and the current shouldn't be too strong there."

"Sounds right, Chris," I said. He was thinking well.

"Got it," said Margaret.

"Okay. So first, we do the same thing we just did, straight back. Once we're untied, we face the other way and row for the sandbar. All right? Here we go! One, two, three, now!"

We got the dinghies moving again and brought them up to the coral head.

"Tell me when we're right on top of it, Dad! I want to take us a little beyond."

"Almost..." I said. "Now."

"Okay, let's keep going, keep going, you all set, Margaret?"

"Yes," she said, rising to her knees.

"Okay, now!"

She dove over the side and, twenty seconds later, re-surfaced, gasping for air. I was paddling hard, twisted around to watch, as she hauled herself up on the gunwale. She rolled in and Chris yelled, "Go!"

I turned around on my knees and sliced the mast into the sea on the side away from the sandbar, then again, and the dinghies, chased by the current, began to move starboard, too. Margaret had scrambled to the bow of the Avon, dropped down on Chris's right and started to paddle furiously with her right arm. I stared at their backs as I stroked. The three of us bent to it.

Come on. Come on. Let's do it. Come on. My head was down and I was paddling as fast as I could. The current was trying hard to take us to past the little sandbar. I kept my pole on my left, to port. It was maddening to feel how little resistance the sea gave it. Like I was not making much of a difference. I tried to get more strokes in, one a second, even. My arms started to ache.

I looked up to get my bearings. I was getting a little dizzy. We were closer, but it still looked awfully far.

We were close, pretty close but almost past. I put my head back down, dug in again and — the dinghies really moved forward. Another quick stroke, more response! We were angling sharper in toward it, too. The lee! We were entering the lee! The water was getting lighter blue. Through the ache in my arms and back, I looked up and saw the shore twenty feet off. I bent to it again. It was almost mindless now. Survive. The beach was life. I looked up again. The water was shallow in front of me. Could we get out? No, not yet. Paddle. Hard. Get there. The pole scraped on a coral head.

Chris surged up and dropped over the bow into a foot of water. Facing the dinghies, he threw the Avon's painter over his left shoulder and reached back with his right hand, pulling the end round his hip. Digging his feet in, he pulled the dinghies forward to the beach. The beach! I paddled hard, striking another coral head and pushing off it. Margaret dropped over the bow and gave the Avon a pull. Again I dug the paddle into the water and I heard the crunch as the bow of the Avon hit sand. I flopped over the side and, on all fours, grabbed the Sandpiper and yanked it forward. Margaret was kneeling on the sand. "Land," she gasped. "It feels — so good."

She tried to get to her feet but her legs buckled under her. She looked at us with dismay. "My legs don't work."

A tiny wave broke at the back of the Avon and washed over us, then sucked at us a little as it moved back out. Chris, on his knees now too, pulled the stern of the soft dinghy sideways, up onto the beach, bringing the hard dinghy with it. I took the bow of the Sandpiper and pulled, crawling. We got both well beached. The three of us crawled up to dry sand. Collapsed. It was actually dry. It was unbelievably good.

My body felt like it was still moving over the waves. Like when you first get off skates. Oh, it was good to lie in the lowering sun. I was even getting a little dry. I hadn't been dry for a long time. I thanked God for the warming sun, as I'd thanked Him for a score of things already.

Was there any water? Chris and Margaret were moving about a bit. I got to my knees, tried to stand, but my legs wouldn't support me. I crawled about twenty feet up the beach and lay down again. A hermit crab crawled by me. I grabbed it, pulled it out of its shell and gulped it down. Yuk, it was slimy. But, I was hungry. Soon, Chris and Margaret, on their knees, dragged the Avon up to where I was.

"Is there any water?" I asked.

"We'll look," he said. "We want to prop this up with the oar and you can lay under it."

They did that and went back to the shoreline to drag up the Sandpiper. Chris was walking a little, now. When they got back to me I asked Margaret how her legs were.

"They're so swollen, I didn't realize how swollen they were. There's no strength in them." She tried to stand again, got to her feet, stood there wobbling like a new-born colt. "We've got to take a look around. Find water."

"Can you make it, Margaret?" Chris asked her.

"I'll make it."

"Look at those rain clouds," I said. There were clouds heading in our direction. This was hopeful. "Suppose you wipe out the Sandpiper with our shirts and maybe we can catch rain in it. Maybe a lot of rain."

"Good idea, Bob," said Margaret. "Chris, let's take it back down to the water and rinse it out before we wipe it. It's pretty dirty in there."

After that, they set the hard dinghy near me, right side up, facing the skies. While they were off searching the sandbar, I scooped out my own length in the sand underneath the Avon, to about six inches deep; still nice dry sand. I lay under the propped up dinghy; the dugout gave me a feeling of security. I was weak as a baby, here was my blanket. And somehow I felt sure the Sandpiper would soon be sloshing with lots and lots of rainwater. We could bend into it and drink and drink. All the water we wanted, all we needed.

They came back with eggs. "That low-lying stuff that we thought maybe was scrub?" said Chris. "It was a flock of birds. Boobies, terns, seagulls, lots of things."

Margaret eyed the rainclouds. "Do they look like they're passing?" I looked out from the cover of the Avon. They were passing to the north. They were up there, full of water, drifting past, holding their water in, not giving us the life they could — giving us nothing.

"Did you try the eggs while you were getting them?"

"We shared one. It was fine."

They handed one to me, and I cracked it open. It was about the size of a chicken egg. I poured the whole thing into my mouth. Didn't have much taste. Immediately it felt funny to have something in my stomach. I cracked open another one and swallowed it while Chris and Margaret did

the same. I cracked another, looked at it, and couldn't eat it.
I felt my stomach couldn't fit it. Down there was a solid
knot, and the eggs made me feel very full, overfull.
Margaret stopped after two, herself. Chris had three.

We all slept a bit.

"Bob, wake up," Margaret said. "We have to get farther
up the beach. The tide'll be coming in."

"Hey, I dug this whole thing out."

"The tide will soak us."

"Chris, don't you think this is high enough?"

"I don't know, Dad."

"You don't know? You're in charge, aren't you?"

"Oh, I don't know."

"Bob, it's not high enough. We have to move."

I thought, I'm not digging another stupid hole. Then I
thought, I don't want to argue with her. Maybe she'll just
let me stay here.

Margaret looked at me for a moment. She looked
concerned, frightened even. Then she pulled the Avon off
the oar and started dragging it up the beach. Chris popped
the oar out of the sand and followed her, taking one side of
the dinghy and helping her drag it. I looked after them,
angry. Then I rolled over, got to my knees, got to my feet,
wobbling like crazy. I stood for a moment, took a step, took
another, rested my legs. Started off again, three steps and
rest; five steps and rest. By the time I was up to ten steps, I
paused and looked up to where Margaret was scooping out a

new dugout on higher ground. I was walking. And she was a big part of the reason.

9:30 p.m.
Colin Busch home
Kawa Kawa, Bay of Islands
New Zealand

Janice came into the room and saw that Colin, on the radio, was listening to someone give a weather report in a breezy, happy manner.

"There's a phone call for you, luv."

Colin looked up. "Can I call them back after the net?"

"It's Miller from Search and Rescue."

"I'll take it," he said.

Whipping off his headphones and rising, he dashed to the bedroom phone and picked up the waiting receiver. "Mr. Miller — Any news?"

"Nothing good, I'm afraid, Mr. Busch. But I thought you'd like to know what the plane was doing."

He found it impossible to keep the disappointment out of his voice. "I certainly would. Thanks."

"They were up for a total of fourteen hours. They were able to devote a full twelve hours of that time to intensive visual search. They've landed now at Fiji. During that time, well, they set out from here at nine a.m., on watch right from the start on the chance that the *Vamonos* was limping into harbor. They proceeded at very low altitude to inspect each of the Kermadec Islands and their respective reefs and lagoons. Then they went north to Minerva Reef and up into Tonga. They did an especially thorough search there as that was the most likely area, according to all calculations."

"Do you know these men, Mr. Miller?"

"I know Johnston, the captain. Good man, conscientious, dedicated. I think we can feel quite confident that a capable job was done. For instance, even with all those islands in the Tonga group, they checked some of them more than once. Complete visual search. So, after Tonga, they turned east and followed a zig-zag path toward Beveridge Reef. They had quite a bit of trouble finding it, but find it they did."

"Oh. I'm happy about that. Did they see anything?"

"Yes. They saw the wreckage of a boat, about the size of *Vamonos*. It was too badly damaged to identify it for certain."

"All right then, and what about Haran Reef?'

"They tried to find that as well, but couldn't. Still, they searched the general area. By then, they were starting to get low on fuel, so they searched their way back to Fiji, on the idea that your friends might have gone through Tonga and continued. The aircraft landed there at nightfall."

"Did you talk to the skipper yourself? Was he satisfied?"

"He phoned me from Fiji, yes. He's quite convinced that if there had been anybody trying to get their attention, they would have been spotted. Also that there was nothing to find in the whole area of Tonga, or they would have found it."

"I see."

"But he requested that he be allowed to search the eastern group of Fiji. That was the only area that they hadn't done really thoroughly and, naturally, it's possible to drift through Tonga and on to Fiji. That eastern side would be the first area one would get to."

"He requested this. And?"

"And I authorized a five hour search tomorrow morning. He feels he can get the job done in that time, then return home."

"That was good of you, Mr. Miller. Very good of you. I'm grateful."

"I want to help. I've wanted to all along, Mr. Busch."

SEVENTEEN

What's this strange sensation? Have the waves stopped? How could...

I opened my eyes and was shocked to see the dinghy above me, shading the morning sun. Something lurched in my chest — the world had shifted. Wait. The sandbar! The sand was dry beneath me. What a feeling.

But so thirsty. I propped myself up on my elbow and reached for one of the bird eggs. Cracked it. It had a slightly formed embryo in it. I swallowed it.

Margaret and Chris were beside me, starting to waken. We had a trench for ourselves, a foot deep, that we lay in side by side.

Margaret said, "We're really here..." She yawned, smiled, and said, "Wasn't it wonderful to sleep like that?" I gave her a little smile and lay myself back down again. Weak.

Tiny pincers nipped one of my toes. Quickly I buried my foot in the sand beyond it. Sand crab. Right, they had been nipping me all night. Annoying. We might be on land, but we were far from the comforts of home. Or even of a shack.

The boils were still bad, of course. Worse than ever. I'd slept on my stomach and side, less painful than lying on my back and bottom. I should take my pants off, lie with my butt to the sun. It'd feel good. But I'm so... weary.

Margaret had slid out from under the Avon and now she was saying, "Bob. Chris. Come out, but do it carefully. Don't knock the dinghy." We got ourselves out without mishap and Margaret pointed to the slanted surface of the Avon. "Dew," she said. She put her chin on the side nearest her, put her tongue out and down, and a little pool of fresh water ran down to her. Chris tried it, careful not to sway the surface, and got his reward. Then I did. We continued to take turns until all the tiny pools had been drunk. It wasn't much but it was fresh water. The first in four days. It was quite a find.

Chris started taking off his clothes. I realized how awful mine felt. Damp, crusty things. I started to take my rags off.

"That's a good idea," said Margaret. She took off her shirt. It struck me how amazing it was that all three of us could stand around stark naked without a single thought of modesty or shame.

"Now for the hard part," she said, with a wry grin. She undid her trousers and started to work them down. "Oh!" she cried, the narrow waistband squeezing her bottom. She continued to wince and work the pants down. When she got them to thigh-level, she pushed them quickly to her knees.

Chris, behind her, groaned, "Oh, Margaret..." From where I was standing, I saw that her thighs were completely covered with boils. She looked down and her mouth opened. Her legs had been covered by the jeans for twenty-three days. Margaret pushed the pants to her ankles and sat down painfully in the sand to take them off.

"Ohhh... My ankles... My ankles look like when you cook a turkey and the skin swells so tight..."

I wanted to do something and felt a surge of anger that there was nothing I could do. Nothing that would make any real difference. "Do you still have the needle, honey?" I asked.

"Yes, in my shirt," she answered.

"I'll help you with them," I said.

Chris, naked, walked off to be on his own. Later, Margaret said, "I can walk. I'm gonna walk around," and she set off in a different direction after putting her clothes on for protection.

It felt so odd to be by myself. Three weeks and more we'd been jammed into that little dinghy. "In each other's pockets," as they say. That's why the others had gone off by themselves. They felt it too. A relief to have some space.

For the first time in so long I could whisper something — and no one could hear it.

Starvation: Inanition. Treatment. In the early stages of rehabilitation, food intake must be limited until gastro-intestinal function has been restored.

— *The Merck Manual*, Sixteenth Edition

In prolonged fasting, the ability to digest food may be impaired or lost entirely because the stomach gradually stops secreting digestive juices.

— *American Medical Association Encyclopedia of Medicine*

The sandy side of the sandbar was the leeward side. It stretched down to a tiny lagoon where we'd landed. The water gradually deepened and became the vastness of the Pacific. The other side was shale. I gingerly got to my feet. I was wobbly, but I could stand. I started down toward the lagoon. The sand had some shale in it, naturally, and broken seashells, and I planned each step I took before I made it; my feet were very tender. We hadn't walked on our feet for over three weeks.

Halfway down, about thirty feet, I stopped to rest. I stood staring at four islands out there. The closest seemed ten or twelve miles away. It looked lush. It looked like life, but the sea intervened.

The egg in my stomach didn't feel good, as uncomfortable as the ones the day before. Perhaps we should kill one of the boobies. But the thought of the raw, stringy meat going into my belly was repulsive. I walked, shaking a little at the knees, around to my left toward the windward side. Shale. Sharp. I wouldn't go that far. Hundreds of birds over there.

Cawing, peeping, shrieking. A bunch of their wings flapped from time to time with a cracking like firecrackers. The breeze blew steadily on my face, not too strongly, as it was morning. I thought about all the time we'd been in the dinghies, struggling to survive. Out the windward side would be where we'd come from. We'd come all that way, probably seven hundred miles, for this had to be Fiji. To a little rock in the ocean. This forlorn, barren place. Where we would die.

I felt exhausted. I sank to my knees and started crawling back to the Avon.

---

10 A.M.
Orion aircraft
Just out of Nadi Airport, Fiji
Captain Johnston commanding

"Gentlemen, now that we're in the air, I'd like to suggest to you that you may not be home for dinner tonight. As highly trained and experienced as you are, I'm sure you'll agree with me that searching for a life raft in a vast ocean is an arduous business, would you not?"

The crew, a little bewildered, voiced their agreement.

"An arduous business," the captain repeated. "And often quite time-consuming. I've seen five hours pass in a flash. In fact, eight, nine, ten hours. Passes in a flash. Anyone else familiar with that phenomenon?"

"Yep, Captain. I think we're all agreed."

———————————

"Those rain clouds are just drifting right on by," I said. The skies on three sides of us were dark and fat with water. Most of the sky had dark streaks sweeping down into the ocean; it was raining out there.

We sat staring up at the clouds, breezes blowing over us, our jackets over our shoulders, the three of us together again in our dugout. The Avon was down next to us, the sun being behind the masses of cloud. The Sandpiper faced the sky nearby us, ready to catch rain. Futility.

Chris reached for an egg, and I followed suit. Margaret was sitting next to Chris, and, as he cracked his open, she said, "Hold it, guys."

I said, "What?" and cracked mine open.

"Chris's egg has a chickie starting."

"Yeah, this one too," I said.

"Well, let's not eat the ones that do. There are plenty of eggs."

"What's the difference?" Chris said, annoyed.

"If they're forming, they might have blood." This is an important point in our view of the Scriptures. We don't eat blood; it's sacred. That's why we'd bled the booby bird before eating it.

"They don't have blood, yet," said Chris, and tipped it into his mouth.

"Chris," I said. "She has a point, maybe they do."

His foot jumped back as a sand crab bit him. He leaned

forward, snatched it out of the sand, and said to it, "That's the last toe you're gonna bite." He popped it in his mouth. Got up chewing and walked away.

"We really shouldn't eat the embryos, Bob."

"All right, Margaret."

"I'll tell you what. Those old, washed up coconuts I found may be good for this. Once I get them open, we can use them for bowls. Then I'll separate out the chick parts and pour the rest into the coconut shells."

"Okay."

She picked herself up and walked back down to the shore. She'd been having a time of it, getting them open without an ax. She'd soaked them, then peeled them strip by strip, soaking again and again. She was trying to get to the round, brown coconut heart. She'd spent two hours on them already. It'd take hours more. Where would she get the energy? And if the sun came out again, it was very hot work, too. Then she'd have to find a way to crack them. A sand crab bit my toe. I reached over, plucked it out of the sand, and ate it.

———————

Margaret had done it. She'd brought the bare brown coconuts up to the dugout, gathered the biggest stones she could and, using seashells, had cracked them open and got us four rough halves. The coconut shells contained no water or milk any more, of course. The liquid had turned to sponge. Faintly moist. The meat was very hard, completely dried out. With a shell, Margaret cut the sponge up and we ate two thirds of it, saving one-third for Chris. She cracked off some bits of the meat. It was difficult but we chewed and swallowed them.

"Bob, I'm worried about Chris. He's not so terribly thin as you but he's definitely skinny. His eyes are sunken. And he doesn't seem to be the old Chris. Definitely not the one of a couple of days ago, taking responsibility for the boats."

"He doesn't say much."

"No. No, he doesn't. I'm gonna talk to him."

She walked off but returned a few minutes later. My eyes hurt and I kept them closed.

"He was lying in the sun. I said to him, 'Chris, the sun's too strong now, put on some clothes.' Do you know what he said? 'What's the difference?' He's... apathetic."

"He thinks he's going to die."

"Well, he's not going to die — We'll do everything we humanly can. No one is going to die."

I opened my eyes and looked over at her. What could she do to prevent it? "I'm so sorry I got us into this, honey," I said. "I'm so sorry." She leaned over and kissed my cheek.

In the afternoon, I got to my feet and walked off to the left once more. My leg muscles hurt now but I was a little surer on my feet. I still planned every step. My feet were getting sore regardless. After a bit, the sand began to have too much shale mixed into it and was starting to pebble out. I reached the shale table that Margaret had mentioned finding, and I sat down on one of its "benches." Long slabs of shale, dense, almost like concrete. Must have taken several natives to carry each piece and set this up. Which island were they from? Was this a regular place for them to come? Certainly not much of a picnic spot. Was it a rest stop on the way somewhere? Did they come for the birds or the eggs?

How often would they come? Maybe they came every week. Maybe it was a regular thing. Maybe they came once a year. Maybe they used to come, but not anymore.

I wonder when we'll die. The sun felt good on my body.

I looked up to see Chris walking slowly in my general direction. I caught his eye and he changed direction toward me. When he got near, he said, "Hi," sounding tired.

"What've you been doing?" I asked him.

"Nothing. Looking for food. Sittin' around."

"What did you find? Anything?"

"Sand crabs. They're all over the place." He squatted and scooped through the sand at his feet. He turned up, not a sand crab, but a hermit crab. A thrill of ill-remembered fear passed through me. He picked up the shell and plucked out the crab. "Want half?" He held it up to me. I bit the creature in half. It was mushy, like a snail. I swallowed it.

We walked a little ways back. I said, "You've got Margaret worried. She thinks you're really down."

"I am really down."

"She thinks that if you let your spirits sink, if you give up, you'll die."

He didn't say anything to that.

"Anything special? Or just the whole mess?"

"The whole thing."

"Margaret really cares about you, you know."

"Margaret's great," he said listlessly. "She's tough. And she's always trying to be cheery, now. For us. But that's not gonna make any difference, you know."

I didn't know what to say. I felt the same way, but I somehow didn't want him to feel like that. He stared at his feet.

"Nothing's certain," I tried. "We may get out of this. Jehovah may want us to, in the end."

"Why not now? And why not a week ago, or two weeks?" He looked quickly up at me, then down again. His face had worn a grimace of pain, and not physical pain. "Why should anything change?"

"I don't know, Christian. A month ago I'm sure I would have had a good, sensible, strong answer ready. A month ago I was sure of myself. Now the only thing I have left is my faith. I don't have an answer for you."

My son looked up at my face. Pain still, yes, but maybe it had eased a little. A moment went by. Then he said, "That's okay, Dad."

11:30 p.m.
Colin Busch home
Kawa Kawa, Bay of Islands
New Zealand

Colin slowly dialed the number he'd been given. A tired male voice answered. Colin asked, "Is this Captain Johnston?"

"Yes, it is."

"I'm Colin Busch, the land-based radio operator who

instigated Mr. Miller's calling for this search. He gave me your number. I just wanted to thank you."

"Let me assure you Mr. Busch — We tried out there."

"I'm sure you did, Captain. You and your crew both. Mr. Miller told me about you requesting the additional search today."

"What Mr. Miller is not quite informed about, and I'd appreciate it if you kept this between ourselves, is that we took off at six a.m. for a five hour search and made it back over the Bay of Islands at eight this evening. Fourteen hours. I was just so sure they were out there. We searched that eastern group so thoroughly. We figured, you know, that if they'd wrecked on a reef, they're going to be in a life raft, which wouldn't come up on our shipboard radar, so we didn't depend on that. It was a visual from beginning to end. We're well trained at this, we take shifts scanning to keep ourselves sharp and we do this thing for hours on end all the time. We saw nothing. Then we searched our way back to New Zealand, swinging in a wide zig-zag. We ran the aircraft to its maximum endurance, both days. I really thought we'd find them."

"I really thought so, too. But maybe that was because the only other possibility is that... they're dead."

"I'd go out again if they'd let me, but they can't. Not without some new information. The search was thorough. It was based on the information we had. You can never be positive you searched under every rock but — we're convinced that they couldn't have been out there."

"Yes." There was a pause. "Thank you again, Captain. Please thank your crew."

EIGHTEEN

Day twenty-five
December 4, 1982
Nunuku sandbar
Lau Group
Eastern Division, Fiji

I turned over onto my back, waking, and felt my stomach lurch painfully. My eyes popped open. Diarrhea! I realized I was going to release my bowels right there. I clamped down on the sphincter muscle and scrambled to my knees, then my feet, and scuttled a little way down the beach. Pain in my stomach, sweat on my face. I released the sphincter and just a small amount of liquid bubbled quickly out, running down my naked thigh. I felt miserable. The pain receded just a little.

I looked up at the dugout and saw Chris heading off. Another sharp pain hit my lower stomach, but nothing more came out. My first bowel movement since day one in the dinghies.

With my foot, I pushed sand over some drops that had reached the ground, then headed slowly down to the water.

Wading in up to my thighs, I crouched in the water and cleaned my self with my hand. Then I cleaned my hand in the ocean bed. Soon Chris came down to the water as well.

I returned, exhausted, to the Avon, where Margaret told me she had a stomach ache.

"Ache or sharp pain?" I asked.

"Sort of a dull ache," she answered.

"I had sharp pain, then diarrhea," I said, sitting, weak.

"Maybe it's the protein," she said. "We've been on a minimal diet, a vegetable and fruit diet. The bird eggs are mostly protein."

"Our systems couldn't handle it, I guess," I said. I stretched out and turned to her. "Oh, Margaret. Look at your thighs."

"I know," she said, miserably. There must have been thirty suppurating boils on each leg. The legs were swollen beyond belief, despite the gouging we'd done the day before. Angry sores everywhere.

I couldn't say anything to her. My beautiful wife, her beautiful body — Oh, God, save her. I know I got her into this. Please get her out.

Chris walked up the beach. When he got close, we saw he was carrying what looked like an old liquor bottle. "Look what I found," he said, bringing it close. It contained a blue-green liquid, thick like dehydrated paint. "Wonder what it is." With a strange little sing-song, he said, "I could drink it and se-ee."

"What?" Margaret said.

He twisted the top off and raised it to his lips.

With alarm, she cried, "Chris! You don't know what's in there!"

He looked at her. His eyes were dull but his voice came

out sharp: "It doesn't matter."

"Of course it matters!"

He tossed the bottle away and started to walk off. He stopped and called over his shoulder, wearily, "I'm sorry, Margaret. I didn't mean to get nasty. It's just —" His eyes popped open and he headed for the beach. I saw him squat in the water. Soon, I had another attack of the runs, myself. For some reason, Margaret didn't, but continued to ache.

This went on for an hour. Eventually we gave each other salt water enemas. After that we were better. The same old dull ache of hunger, but at least not the sharp pain of stomach cramp.

———————

"We have to exercise," said Margaret.

She astonished me. Exercise was the last thing I wanted to do. I wanted to husband my strength.

Chris said, "No way. I walk. That's enough."

"I've seen you walk, Chris. You amble. Then you squat like an Aborigine for a while. Then you slowly drag yourself someplace else. Then you lay down and rest."

"I don't want to exercise, Margaret."

"Neither do I," I said.

"I'm not gonna watch you two waste away in front of my eyes. There's almost nothing we can do to change our situation, to survive. But one thing we can do is we can get our circulation going, build up these muscles that we haven't used for over three weeks. We need to take off our clothes and get in the water. Chris, help your father up."

"Margaret —"

"Chris. This is not a game, here. This is our lives I'm talking about. Help your father up."

Chris looked at me, hesitated, then grasped me under one arm. I got to my feet, Margaret took my other arm, and we all started down to the shore. My legs were trembly. I stopped once on the way and rested on my knees. As I was rising again, I put my left hand onto my buttock. Where I'd normally expect to feel fat and muscle, my hand continued in. The cheek had become concave.

When we got to the water, Margaret put her arm around my waist, brought me into the shallows, and said, "Turn around, honey." We got to our knees and she had me push my legs out behind me. "Balance on your elbows and kick. Chris, c'mon, you too." Chris got down into the water and we all kicked. After a minute I rested. They continued. I started up again and heard her say, "Don't stop, Chris. You don't need to rest yet." He did what she told him.

———————

Later that afternoon, I turned to her under the Avon. "We're gonna have to leave."

The thought of getting back into the dinghies filled me with loathing. We were on land and I was so tired. But the bird eggs weren't doing it. The choice seemed inevitably simple. Leave or die.

"I keep praying that someone will come by," she said. "But who knows how long it'll be before anybody does? You know, I was thinking that, because we found that table made of shale, people do come here, but I think you're right. We can't just sit."

"I'll never last. Neither will Chris. We have to try for that near island."

"We'd have to paddle against the current."

"Yes. I'll make a second paddle with that plywood and that broom handle we found. I can use that and Chris can use the oar." Perhaps I could paddle, I wasn't sure.

"We need time to get ready, don't you think? Let's give it 'til tomorrow, say noon. Then, before the afternoon seas pick up, we should go."

"We have to go," I said.

Cikobia-i-Lau
Lau Group
Eastern Division, Fiji

Leonard Tolhurst sat in the comfortable native building, finishing dinner with his wife and Pastor Kepereli Duana, the area resident for the Seventh Day Adventist Church.

"Do you want to come with us, tomorrow, Val?" Leonard asked his wife.

Valerie Tolhurst replied, "Are you kidding? Sit in an open motorboat for, what, six hours? Salt spray and sunburn? No thanks."

He turned to the local pastor with a smile. "She doesn't find shell-collecting quite as compelling as she might."

"Well, I guess we'll have to struggle through without her. Where do you want to go? Have you decided?"

"I certainly want to get to Sovu before we go back home, but let's see how the sea is tomorrow."

"All right, Leonard. The others will want to spearfish, but it's really up to you where we go. You're paying for the fuel."

NuNuku sandbar
Lau Group
Eastern Division, Fiji

Just before sundown, Chris came walking across the sand wearing his red sweatshirt, retrieved from the masthead. He had the hood pulled forward over his face, though the day was still hot. He walked, scanning the ground intently.

"What are you doing?" I asked him as he came up.

"Merlin the Magician. I'm Merlin the Magician." He had a different bottle this time. I could see its raised lettering on the label-less glass: Smirnoff. "I make magic potions." His acne was terrible now, distorting his wonderful face within the hood. He grinned at me.

"What's in the bottle, Chris?"

"My brew. I've been making it all day."

"Making it how?"

"Like this," he said, and pulled a piece of the dry, dry coconut from the flap pocket of the sweatshirt. He put it in his mouth and chewed. Then he brought the bottle to his lips and spat it in. "With some egg and some sea water. And this." He crouched, swept the sand with his hand and revealed a sand crab. Putting it in his mouth, he chewed thoughtfully. Raising the bottle, he let liquid drool into it from between his puckered lips.

He extended the bottle to me. "You can have some. It's magic."

Day twenty-six
December 5, 1982

Around nine a.m. I was sitting under the Avon, using the strong sail thread to bind the broom handle to the plywood. The plywood was less than a foot long, five inches wide.

All the time in the dinghies, we'd resisted and resisted. When we'd made landfall, the relief had been enormous. Now our powers of resistance were not what they were. And we were going right back to where we'd been: sitting in the wet with the boils, watching for the rogue waves — though now, on a beam reach to get to the island, even normal swells could capsize us. Having to paddle and having no strength to do it with.

Chris sat morosely in the sand, his hood pulled forward over his face. He muttered for the third time since dawn, "I don't want to go."

Margaret glanced at him frustratedly. "We have to go. Please go kill that bird for us to take."

"I like it here," he pressed. "We're safe here. We shouldn't go back out."

She got angry. "We said we'd die together. You said it. And it's a much better idea to survive together. I'm not going to bury your father in the sand. And then you."

Chris kept his head down for a moment. Then he got up and headed for the flock of birds.

———————————

Tolhurst party
Five miles WNW of Cikobia-i-Lau

"What do you think, Leonard?" asked Pastor Duana.

Tolhurst stood in the large motor launch, peering through binoculars beyond the reef half a mile ahead of them. "Looks pretty calm out there, Kepereli. I think we should give it a go."

"We can head north a bit and find the American Passage, go through there and out of the lagoon."

"Oh? Why do they call it the American Passage?"

"Well, because it faces northwest, toward the U.S. So, what about Sovu?"

"The sea looks calm today. If we can, I'd like to get to NuNuku before we leave. Sovu is inside the reef: We can see it any day, even if the weather gets rougher. A good chance missed may later be regretted, as they say."

"Right, then." The native pastor turned to the four Fijians who made up the rest of the party and spoke rapidly in their language. The launch altered its course to the north. Turning back to his colleague, also an S.D.A. minister and Chairman of Theology at Fulton College, Fiji, Duana said, "Leonard, I don't completely understand why you want to go to both Sovu and NuNuku. Will the shells be so different on one than the other?"

"I'm told that Sovu is beautiful, so I definitely want to go there, but the NuNuku birds are — You see, a former student of mine, an ornithologist now, camped on NuNuku overnight, a few years back. While there, he banded some chicks. As I was leaving on this trip, he asked me to stop by the atoll, if I could, and check the numbers on the bands, let him know the details. So I'd like to oblige him if I can."

One of the Fijians, sitting easily on the prow, called out to Duana in Fijian.

"He says maybe we can cross the reef here, instead of the American Passage. Save some time if there's enough draft for the keel to get over safely."

Pulling alongside a section of the long reef encircling the group of small islands, they inspected the area which was free of the crashing breakers present for miles up and down. After consultation among themselves, the natives slowly powered across the relatively tranquil spot. The swells picked up quickly on the other side, but only to about three feet, and the boat headed out comfortably.

After a few minutes, the motor launch lifted on a swell and Duana said, "There's NuNuku, we're right on course."

Tolhurst got out his binoculars and looked through them. "Hard to see anything. The boat's pitching too much," he said.

Five minutes further along, another of the Fijians spoke to Duana, who translated, "He says he thinks someone's on the sandbar."

"Why?" asked Tolhurst.

"He says he doesn't know. He has a hunch."

The natives intermittently spoke among themselves as they drew a bit nearer the speck in the ocean.

"Ask them who could be on the sandbar. Do they have any idea?"

Duana spoke to the natives and then his colleague. "They say maybe Japanese fishermen. Poaching."

"Could they be dangerous?"

"Yes, they could be. If that's the case, we should not go there. Oh! Look at that."

"Looks like a flock of birds."

"Yes, it does. I think they're right. Someone is on that island."

"If it's poachers, will we be able to tell?"

"Perhaps. Perhaps from their boat."

Chris had killed the bird before he got back. We'd drained it and gutted it and hung it from the mast. I was laying under the Avon recuperating from the exertion when he said, "I'll get some eggs, too." I couldn't muster myself to answer him. Margaret, sitting up next to me, replied. He went off.

I silently prayed. This would be it. A jolt of adrenal fear jumped in my chest. This would be the last effort. We'd get there or we'd drown. If we were capsized, we'd all die. Chris didn't have the strength to survive that. Not even Margaret would. Me, I might not even be able to get to the boat. I heard a thousand wings beating as the flock took off. Chris had frightened them to flight. After a bit, Chris came back, set the eggs in the sand, sat himself down wearily. Then he lay down. Margaret was checking the rigging.

"Dad?"

"Yes."

"I don't want to face it."

"I know, son."

"It's so warm and comfortable here, after the dinghies."

"But take a look at what you're saying. It's not comfortable here at all. It's a barren coral rock, covered with shale and sand. It's not a living thing. It's dead."

"We can get along here."

"No, we can't. We can only die here." Margaret came over and sat down next to us.

Chris said, "I'm afraid to go out on the sea again."

"Those islands out there are life," I said. "They're grandma and grandpa and your friends in school. They're your chance of growing up, having a chance to do what you want. They're a wife. And kids. They're music and laughter."

"What if we don't make it?"

Margaret said, softly, "Then we'll just drop into sleep. A peaceful sleep, and wait for the resurrection."

"Chris," I said. "We have a chance. We have to take it. We might make it back to life. If we stay here and nobody comes — now listen to me — I'm certain we'll die. Certain of it. We have a chance. We have to take it."

There was silence. Then Margaret, even softer, asked him, "What do you say, Chris?"

"I say... okay."

I put out my hand and took his in mine. After a second, he squeezed it. Margaret took his other hand, and I saw that he squeezed hers too. Margaret turned away to finish preparations. She said, loudly, "What's that?"

I turned my head to her. She got out from under the dinghy and stood up. "What's that?!" she repeated.

Chris got up. He stared where she was pointing.

She shouted, "That's a boat!!"

I propped myself up on my elbows and looked out to sea. I saw a smudge on the water.

"I think... It is a boat," yelled Chris. He and Margaret picked up their jackets. They ran down to the shore waving them, yelling at the top of their lungs, screaming.

The boat seemed to be veering toward the windward side,

yes it was definitely veering off. Didn't they see us?

"Do they see us??" yelled Margaret. She began running toward the shale side of the sandbar, Chris right behind, waving his jacket.

The boat tacked and headed straight toward us. A figure on the launch waved. Chris and Margaret halted and embraced. Looking once more at the boat, sure now that it was heading in, they turned and staggered up the beach toward me. They were crying, though their eyes had no water to give.

I wanted to stand. I struggled up and fell again. I got to my knees. They reached me and dropped down in the sand, hugging me. I cried with my family. We were saved.

EPILOGUE

The phenomenon called El Niño occurs intermittently on our planet. It recurs on average every four or five years but the period between Niños can be as short as two years or as long as ten. Usually they occur in much milder forms than the one which began in late 1982 and reached its peak early in 1983. This massive Niño left more than 1,100 people dead, incalculable numbers of fish and animals destroyed, and damage estimated at $8.7 billion. The alteration of the earth's weather caused drought, floods, fires, and starvation from Australia to the Americas to southern Africa. Originating off the coast of South America, its atmospheric center, "the great red spot", finally came to rest in Tahiti.

Soon after their rescue, Bob, Margaret and Chris Aros were told by the local natives that if they had ventured out in the direction they had planned to, from NuNuku sandbar, they would have encountered the reef that surrounds their island and two others, and would surely have drowned.

The fine and gentle natives of Cikobia-i-Lau immediately opened their village and hearts to the survivors. They kindly fed, bathed, and clothed the Aros family, lay them in their own beds, and watched over them in the night.

Two of the natives, Paul, and Tucana were exceptionally

attentive to the Aros's.

There was a radio on the island and it was used to summon the medical officer from Vanua Balavu, about ten miles away, who brought medicines and supplies over on the government launch.

The medicine was administered by Valerie Tolhurst, Leonard's wife, who was a trained nurse. The ulcerated staph infections were her first concern, and before allowing the Aros's to go to sleep, she applied the antibiotic ointment and bandages which had been brought.

Leonard Tolhurst instructed the radio operator to place additional calls to the Suva police and the American embassy, relaying news of the rescue and phone numbers of the Aros's relatives in the United States.

The following day, the Prime Minister of Fiji hired a private helicopter to airlift the Aros's to Colonial War Memorial Hospital in Suva, on the large island of Viti Levu.

Their attending physician, Dr. Rajan Nandam had to refuse Bob's request that he immediately lance and drain the largest boils, knowing that to do so would, in Bob's state of excessive dehydration, lead to a gangrene infection. He also estimated that Bob Aros, had he not been rescued when he was, would have died within forty-eight hours.

The first night the Aros's spent in the hospital, a nurse identifying herself only as Anila, was moved to compassion by the sight of Margaret's legs. She requested and got permission to return after her shift to massage Margaret Aros's swollen limbs with a medicinal lotion.

Christian Aros brought with him, from NuNuku sandbar, the paddle which had been with them until the end. When asked what he wanted to do first upon getting home, he replied, "Eat some pizza."

Their arrival at Colonial War Memorial Hospital was greeted by newsmen anxious for a press conference. One of the things which all three survivors stressed again and again was that they credited their amazing survival to their faith in God.

During their stay at the hospital, they were visited by members of the local Jehovah's Witnesses congregation who'd heard their interviews on radio. Yachties anchored in Suva harbor, who had never met the Aroses, came to visit. Many other strangers, having heard or read accounts of the experience, appeared during visiting hours day after day.

Colin Busch wrote to the Aroses later, saying, "I can tell you that was certainly a fantastic morning for Jan and me when our bedside radio woke us up and we heard the headlines that a life raft with three Americans had been found. They gave us the headlines before they read the news and, of course, your news item had to be the last one. We waited and waited. Finally they told us what they knew at that point, which wasn't very much, that three Americans off a boat had been found. We thought this simply must be you. A fantastic morning."

By the time the Aroses were found, there were at least twenty yachties in New Zealand who were ham operators and were following the story through the Pacific Maritime Net. When they received the good news that the Aroses had been found, there was an outpouring of exuberance, relief and happiness. A gift was sent to the hospital in Fiji, along with a card that was signed by all.

Leonard Tolhurst recalls in a letter how he had, on the sandbar, heard the Aros's repeatedly saying, "Thank Jehovah," as they wept with their dry tear ducts. He continues, "We discussed freely how we all believed that God had indeed answered their prayers for rescue — we'd nearly gone to another destination."

The Aros's became international news. Photographs of the helicopter landing at Suva and news of the rescue reached the front pages of the world's newspapers, and the story was featured in major news telecasts, particularly in the United States.

Bob and Margaret live happily today in Belmont Shore, California. Chris Aros is married and lives in Kona, Hawaii.

Glossary

Aboard – In the boat.

Adrift – Drifting loose from any stable object.

Afloat – Floating.

Aft – Toward the rear of the boat.

Anchor – Steel device with prongs designed to hold the boat secure to the bottom of the ocean floor. It's attached by a rope or chain to the boat.

Astern – Behind the boat.

Automatic Pilot – Mechanical and electronic device that steers a boat on a pre-determined compass heading.

Awash – When a boats deck, or a reef is washed over by water.

Backstay – A small diameter length of stainless steel wire that helps support the mast. It runs aloft from the stern to the top of the mast.

Bail – To remove water with an object or bucket.

Beam – The widest part of the boats deck.

Below – In the cabin. Lower than the deck.

Berth – A bed where someone sleeps on a boat.

Bilge – The lowest point in the boats interior.

Boat – Any vessel small enough to be carried by a larger vessel called a ship.

Boom – A long shaft attached to the mast near the bottom,

to which the foot of the sail is attached.

Bow – The forward end of the boat.

Bunk – On a boat it is a sleeping bed.

Broad Reach – The point of sailing between a beam reach and a run.

Cabin – A room in a boat.

Chart – A map of a body of water rather than land and it's relative position to land.

Chart Table – A flat surface designed for laying a chart on for navigation.

Cleat – A small metal or plastic devise to which a line under pressure can be secured to by wrapping.

Clevis pin – A non-rusting metal pin that fits into and secures one fitting to another.

Clew – The lower rear end of a jib, or mainsail.

Cockpit – A specific location on the boat which is designed to accommodate the steering tiller or wheel, and the crew that will operate it.

Compass – A glass enclosed device with a magnetized mechanism that floats in a special liquid and points near the North Pole.

Course – The direction the boat is heading.

Crew – Everybody on the boat that is working except the captain or skipper.

Cruise – A time period longer than one day that is spent pleasure boating to a destination.

Current – The horizontal motion of the water which is caused by wind and tide.

Deck – The floor on the top of the boat hull.

Degree – A nautical measure equivalent to sixty nautical miles.

Dinghy – A small, light boat.

Dodger – A canvas spray shield located at the front of the cockpit.

Drift – To be carried by current or wind.

Epirb – A battery operated electronic device that transmits your position or location.

Eye – An opening to which a line can pass through such as an eye bolt.

Fast – To secure. To "make fast".

Fix – A boats position which is determined by two or more bearings from stars, sun or moon.

Flukes – The protruding sharp arms of an anchor that dig in or catch onto the bottom.

Following Sea – Wave from astern or behind the rear of the boat.

Foot – The lower edge of the sail.

Forestay – A small-diameter length of stainless steel wire that helps support the mast. It runs aloft from the bow to the top of the mast.

Forward – Toward the bow or front of the boat.

Freeboard – The height of the topsides of the boat from the water line to the top of the hull.

Galley – A kitchen on a boat.

Genoa/Genny – A jib or forward sail that extends from the forestay to aft, or behind the mast.

Gunwale – The rail of a boat.

Halyard – A line of wire or rope used to raise a sail.

Head – A bathroom on a boat. A toilet.

Heading – A course or direction.

Helm – The position where the wheel or rudder control is located. A boat's steering wheel.

House – The main cabin structure which protrudes above the deck.

Hove to – To back the jib and lash the tiller to leeward – to encourage the boat to lie quietly and to reduce headway.

Inflatable dingy - A small rubber boat with sections inflated with air.

Jib – Simetimes called foresail. A triangular sail that is used between the forestay and the mast.

Jury rig – A hasty make shift solution to a rigging problem.

Keel – A retractable or permanent fin under the hull that provides a straight line direction stability through the water as well as heavy weight to counteract heeling or leaning to far over.

Ketch – A sailboat with two masts. The aftermast being shorter than the forward or main mast. The aftermast must locate forward of the rudder post.

Latitude – A latural distance line parallel to the equater either north or south and measured in degrees.

Lanyard – A small line used to secure something tight.

Lazaret – A storage locker in the cockpit area.

Lifejacket – A vest type jacket filled with buoyant material used to keep it's wearer afloat.

Life preserver – The same as above with the exception that it can take other forms or shapes, such as a cushion.

Liferaft/Lifeboat – An inflatable rubber boat that is designed specifically for survival.

Line – Any length of rope on the boat that is used for a specific purpose.

Longitude – A verticle distance line that runs perpendicular to the equator to measure distance either east or west of the meridan in degree.

Mainsail (mains'l) – The principle sail on the main mast extending aft.

Maritime – Anything to do with activity on the sea.

Mast – The vertical pole standing on the boat to which the sails are attached.

Mayday – International distress signal.

Minute – A nautical measurement equal to one nautical mile.

Mobile Unit- A boat with a ham radio aboard, used to communicate with land units or other mobile units.

Nautical – Pertaining to navigation of boats, ships, and sailors.

Navigation – The science of getting a boat from one point to another.

Navigator – The person on the boat who has the responsibility to calculate the boats position and direction to it's destination.

Oar – A length of rod or pole with a flat wide portion at the end. Used to row a boat.

Painter – A short line attached to the dingy to pull it or tie it to something else.

Pin – A metal object to secure rigging.

Port – The left side of the boat when facing forward.

Priority traffic – When using the radio, it is information from a radio operator that needs to be transmitted first.

Reach – A course crossing the wind.

Reef – To temporarily decrease the sail area by rolling and securing a portion of that sail.

Reef – A pertrusion from the bottom of the ocean caused by volcanic activity / growth of sea life on that substance.

Rogue Wave – A wave that is of a different direction or sequence than the majority of the waves.

Rudder – A flat wide device extending into the water and attached to a steering wheel or tiller which steers the boat.

Sail – A large fabric section of material designed to capture the wind to propell the boat.

Sail Needle – A strong sharp C shaped needle.

Schooner – A fore and aft rigged vessel having two or more masts.

Sextant – A mechanical instrument used to measure the altitude of heavenly bodies. The navigator can then determine the position of the boat by consulting tables from the Nautical Almanac.

Sheet – A rope from a lower corner of a sail to extend it or move it.

Skipper – Another title for the captain.

Sloop – A sailboat with one mast that is located less than one-third of the length of the boat aft of the forestay.

Sole – The floor of a cockpit or cabin.

Stanchions – Upright rods, bolted to the deck. Lifelines would continue through these poles forming a safety rail around the boat.

Starboard – The right side of the boat when facing forward.

Stem – The forward part of the bow.

Stern – The farthest rear end of the boat.